W9-BPE-775

MULTICULTURAL EDUCATION SERIES
JAMES A. BANKS, *Series Editor*

(continued)

TRANSFORMING EDUCATIONAL PATHWAYS FOR CHICANA/O STUDENTS

A Critical Race Feminista Praxis

Dolores Delgado Bernal
Enrique Alemán, Jr.

TEACHERS COLLEGE PRESS

TEACHERS COLLEGE | COLUMBIA UNIVERSITY
NEW YORK AND LONDON

Published by Teachers College Press, 1234 Amsterdam Avenue, New York, NY 10027

Copyright © 2017 by Teachers College, Columbia University

Cover art: *Adelante*, acrylic on canvas, 24" x 24", © Ruby Chacón

All rights reserved. No part of this publication may be reproduced or transmitted in any form or by any means, electronic or mechanical, including photocopy, or any information storage and retrieval system, without permission from the publisher.

Library of Congress Cataloging-in-Publication Data is available at loc.gov

ISBN 978-0-8077-5791-8 (paper)
ISBN 978-0-8077-5792-5 (hardcover)
ISBN 978-0-8077-7504-2 (ebook)

Printed on acid-free paper
Manufactured in the United States of America

24 23 22 21 20 19 18 17   8 7 6 5 4 3 2 1

For my sons, Olin, Izel, and Pixan, and my husband, Octavio—you are my sources of strength and inspiration.

—Dolores

For my children, Diego, Gema, and Nayeli, and for my wife, Sonya—you give my life's work meaning and purpose.

—Enrique

And especially, for all the students and families at Jackson, for sharing your energy and love, and for teaching us about the power of community knowledge and the leadership it takes to strive for educational equity.

—Enrique and Dolores

Contents

SERIES FOREWORD

Adelante is a Spanish word that means "ahead" or "in front" in English. The Adelante program developed by Delgado Bernal and Alemán at the University of Utah was designed to enable Chican@Latin@[1] students, other students of color, and low-income students to attain the knowledge, skills, and motivation to enroll and succeed in college, and consequently to move "ahead" in their educational aspirations and trajectories. The program was launched in 2005 as a university–school–community partnership in a dual-immersion kindergarten classroom and now extends from kindergarten to the 8th grade. In this book, Delgado Bernal and Alemán examine and reflect on the educational effects of Adelante on the students after a decade of its implementation. They also describe its effects on the culture of Jackson Elementary School, on the teachers, and on the community in which Jackson Elementary School is embedded.

One of the strengths of this readable and informative book is that the authors chronicle the ways in which the Adelante intervention project has been successful as well as the challenges that remain after a decade of work. A significant challenge described vividly by the authors is the persistence of the legacy of institutionalized racism and colonization that casts a long shadow on the educational experiences and trajectories of students of color. This legacy exists not only in Utah but throughout the nation, and it has been documented by myriad scholars and researchers, such as Bigler and Hughes (2009), Leonardo (2013), Lewis (2004), and Lewis and Diamond (2015).

Delgado Bernal and Alemán drew upon Anzaldúan Chicana feminist theories (Anzaldúa, 1987, 1990) and critical race theory (Ladson-Billings & Tate, 1997) when they constructed the "critical race feminista praxis" theoretical framework that undergirds this book and the Adelante project. The authors view their theoretical work and educational interventions as counternarratives to the cultural deficit theories that are institutionalized within schools and universities and that have detrimental effects on the education of Chican@Latin@ students and other students of color. Delgado Bernal and Alemán state that their scholarship and work create "transformative ruptures" that increase educational equality for students of color and low-income students.

The development and implementation of educational interventions based on transformative frameworks and paradigms (Kuhn, 1970)—such as the critical race feminista praxis formulated by Delgado Bernal and Alemán—are essential for low-income students and students of color to attain academic success and educational mobility. The genetic and cultural deficit paradigms have reigned supreme in educational research and practice since IQ testing became popular in the United States during the first decades of the 1900s. These paradigms have detrimental effects on the education and schooling of low-income students and students of color. Although the genetic paradigm is no longer a legitimate conception within most educational research and professional organizations, it still influences educational theory, research, and practice because it is deeply rooted in American social science and education as well as in the popular imagination (Herrnstein & Murray, 1994; Jensen, 1969). The cultural deprivation paradigm, which was formulated and influential during the 1960s and early 1970s (Riessman, 1962), was harshly criticized in the 1970s and 1980s (Baratz & Baratz, 1970; Ginsburg, 1972). However, it re-emerged in a robust way during the 1990s and 2000s, epitomized by the publication and substantial influence among school practitioners of *A Framework for Understanding Poverty* by Ruby K. Payne (1996).

The construction of innovative paradigms and interventions that initiate "transformative ruptures" that increase the academic achievement and educational aspiration of students of color are especially timely and needed because of the growing population of students from diverse racial, ethnic, cultural, linguistic, and religious groups who are attending schools in the United States. Although students in the United States are becoming increasingly diverse, most of the nation's teachers are White, female, and monolingual. Race and institutionalized racism are significant factors that influence and mediate the interactions of students and teachers from diverse groups (G. R. Howard, 2016; T. C. Howard, 2010; Leonardo, 2013). The growing income gap between adults (Stiglitz, 2012)—as well as the gap between youth that is described by Putnam (2015) in *Our Kids: The American Dream in Crisis*—is another significant reason why it is important to help teachers understand how factors such as race and class influence classroom interactions and student learning and to comprehend the ways in which these variables influence student aspirations and academic engagement (Suárez-Orozco, Pimentel, & Martin, 2009).

American classrooms are experiencing the largest influx of immigrant students since the beginning of the 20th century. Approximately 21.5

million new immigrants–documented and undocumented–settled in the United States in the years from 2000 to 2015. Less than 10% came from nations in Europe. Most came from Mexico, nations in South Asia, East Asia, Latin America, the Caribbean, and Central America (Camarota, 2011, 2016). The influence of an increasingly diverse population on U.S. schools, colleges, and universities is and will continue to be enormous.

Schools in the United States are more diverse today than they have been since the early 1900s when a multitude of immigrants entered the United States from Southern, Central, and Eastern Europe. In 2014, the National Center for Education Statistics estimated that the percentage of students from ethnic minority groups made up more than 50% of the students in prekindergarten through 12th grade in public schools, an increase from 40% in 2001 (National Center for Education Statistics, 2014). Language and religious diversity is also increasing in the U.S. student population. The 2012 American Community Survey estimated that 21% of Americans aged 5 and above (61.9 million) spoke a language other than English at home (U. S. Census Bureau, 2012). Harvard professor Diana L. Eck (2001) calls the United States the "most religiously diverse nation on earth" (p. 4). Islam is now the fastest-growing religion in the United States, as well as in several European nations such as France, the United Kingdom, and the Netherlands (Banks, 2009; O'Brien, 2016).

The major purpose of the Multicultural Education Series is to provide preservice educators, practicing educators, graduate students, scholars, and policymakers with an interrelated and comprehensive set of books that summarizes and analyzes important research, theory, and practice related to the education of ethnic, racial, cultural, and linguistic groups in the United States and the education of mainstream students about diversity. The dimensions of multicultural education, developed by Banks (2004) and described in the *Handbook of Research on Multicultural Education* and in the *Encyclopedia of Diversity in Education* (Banks, 2012), provide the conceptual framework for the development of the publications in the series. The dimensions are content integration, the knowledge construction process, prejudice reduction, equity pedagogy, and an empowering institutional culture and social structure. The books in the Multicultural Education Series provide research, theoretical, and practical knowledge about the behaviors and learning characteristics of students of color (Conchas & Vigil, 2012; Lee, 2007), language minority students (Gándara & Hopkins, 2010; Valdés, 2001; Valdés, Capitelli, & Alvarez, 2011), low-income students (Gorski, 2013; Cookson, 2013), and other minoritized population groups, such as students who speak different varieties of English (Hudley & Mallinson, 2011), and LGBTQ youth (Mayo, 2014).

One of the most important and appealing characteristics of the Adelante Partnership is that it initiates the creation of a "college-going culture" in kindergarten classrooms that are populated by low-income and minoritized students, most of whom have parents who have not attended a college or university. The evidence from the authors' interviews and *platicas* (talks) with the students indicate that the various components of the Adelante project—such as university visits, mentoring by university students of color, and academic and cultural enrichment—enable the students in the program to envision themselves as future university students and to identify possible barriers to going to college and ways in which these obstacles may be overcome. The Adelante intervention project helps students to acquire faith in their abilities and the will to succeed. Mary McLeod Bethune, the eminent African American educator, described the power of faith: "Without faith, nothing is possible. With it, nothing is impossible."

—James A. Banks

NOTE

1. I am following the authors' use of Chican@Latin@ to "recognize gender fluidity and to challenge the gender hierarchy and binary present in the Spanish language (the use of the masculine *o* at the end of words to refer to both males and females)" (p. 1, note 2). The authors use *Chicanos* when referring to males only and *Chicanas* when referring to females only.

REFERENCES

Anzaldúa, G. (1987). *Borderlands/la frontera: The new mestizo*. San Francisco, CA: Spinsters/Aunt Lute Books.

Anzaldúa, G. (Ed.). (1990). *Making face, making soul/Haciendo caras: Creative and critical perspectives by women of color*. San Francisco, CA: Aunt Lute Books.

Banks, J. A. (2004). Multicultural education: Historical development, dimensions, and practice. In J. A. Banks & C. A. M. Banks (Eds.), *Handbook of research on multicultural education* (2nd ed., pp. 3–29). San Francisco, CA: Jossey-Bass.

Banks, J. A. (Ed.). (2009). *The Routledge international companion to multicultural education*. New York, NY and London, England: Routledge.

Banks, J. A. (2012). Multicultural education: Dimensions of. In J. A. Banks (Ed). *Encyclopedia of diversity in education* (Vol. 3, pp. 1538–1547). Thousand Oaks, CA: Sage Publications.

Baratz, S. A., & Baratz, J. C. (1970). Early childhood intervention: The social science base of institutionalized racism. *Harvard Educational Review*, *40*(1), 29–50.

Bigler, R. S., & Hughes, J. M. (2009). The nature and origin of children's racial attitudes. In J. A. Banks (Ed.), *The Routledge international companion to multicultural education* (pp. 186–198). New York, NY: Routledge.

Camarota, S. A. (2011, October). *A record-setting decade of immigration: 2000 to 2010.* Washington, DC: Center for Immigration Studies. Retrieved from cis.org/2000-2010-record-setting-decade-of-immigration

Camarota, S. A. (2016, June). *New data: Immigration surged in 2014 and 2015.* Washington, DC: Center for Immigration Studies. Retrieved from cis.org/New-Data Immigration-Surged-in-2014-and-2015

Conchas, G. Q., & Vigil, J. D. (2012). *Streetsmart schoolsmart: Urban poverty and the education of adolescent boys.* New York, NY: Teachers College Press.

Cookson, P. W., Jr. (2013). *Class rules: Exposing inequality in American high schools.* New York, NY: Teachers College Press.

Eck, D. L. (2001). *A new religious America: How a "Christian country" has become the world's most religiously diverse nation.* New York, NY: HarperSanFrancisco.

Gándara, P., & Hopkins, M. (Eds.). (2010). *Forbidden language: English language learners and restrictive language policies.* New York, NY: Teachers College Press.

Ginsburg, H. (1972). *The myth of the deprived child: Poor children's intellect and education.* Englewood Cliffs, NJ: Prentice-Hall.

Gorski, P. C. (2013). *Reaching and teaching students in poverty: Strategies for erasing the opportunity gap.* New York, NY: Teachers College Press.

Herrnstein, R. J., & Murray, C. (1994). *The bell curve: Intelligence and class structure in American life.* New York, NY: The Free Press.

Howard, G. R. (2016). *We can't teach what we don't know: White teachers, multiracial schools* (3rd ed.). New York, NY: Teachers College Press.

Howard, T. C. (2010). *Why race and culture matter in schools: Closing the achievement gap in America's classrooms.* New York, NY: Teachers College Press.

Hudley, A. H. C., & Mallinson, C. (2011). *Understanding language variation in U. S. Schools.* New York, NY: Teachers College Press.

Jensen, A. R. (1969). How much can we boost IQ and scholastic achievement? *Harvard Educational Review*, *39*(1), 1–123.

Kuhn, T. F. (1970). *The structure of scientific revolutions* (2nd ed., enlarged). Chicago, IL: University of Chicago Press.

Ladson-Billings, G., & Tate, W. (1997). Toward a critical race theory in education. *Teachers College Record*, *97*(1), 47–68.

Lee, C. D. (2007). *Culture, literacy, and learning: Taking bloom in the midst of the whirlwind.* New York, NY: Teachers College Press.

Leonardo, Z. (2013). *Race frameworks: A multidimensional theory of racism and education.* New York, NY: Teachers College Press.

Lewis, A. E. (2004). *Race in the schoolyard: Negotiating the color line in classrooms and communities.* New Brunswick, NJ: Rutgers University Press.

Lewis, A. E., & Diamond, J. B. (2015). *Despite the best of intentions: How racial inequality thrives in good schools.* New York, NY: Oxford University Press.

Mayo, C. (2014). *LGBTQ youth and education: Policies and practices.* New York, NY: Teachers College Press.

National Center for Education Statistics. (2014). *The condition of education 2014.* Retrieved from nces.ed.gov/pubs2014/2014083.pdf

O'Brien, P. (2016). *The Muslim question in Europe: Political controversies and public philosophies.* Philadelphia, PA: Temple University Press.

Payne, R. K. (1996). *A framework for understanding poverty* (4th rev. ed.). Highlands, TX: aha! Process.

Putnam, R. D. (2015). *Our kids: The American dream in crisis.* New York, NY: Simon & Schuster.

Riessman, F. (1962). *The culturally deprived child.* New York, NY: Harper.

Stiglitz, J. E. (2012). *The price of inequality: How today's divided society endangers our future.* New York, NY: Norton.

Suárez-Orozco, C., Pimentel, A., & Martin, M. (2009). The significance of relationships: Academic engagement and achievement among newcomer immigrant youth. *Teachers College Record, 111*(3), 712–749.

U. S. Census Bureau. (2012). *Selected social characteristics in the United States: 2012 American Community Survey 1-year estimates.* Retrieved from factfinder2.census.gov/faces/tableservices/jsf/pages/productview.xhtml?pid=ACS_12_1YR_DP02&prodType=table

U. S. Department of Education. (2009, November). *Race to the Top Program, executive summary.* Retrieved from www2.ed.gov/programs/racetothetop/executive-summary.pdf

Valdés, G. (2001). *Learning and not learning English: Latino students in American schools.* New York, NY: Teachers College Press.

Valdés, G., Capitelli, S., & Alvarez, L. (2011). *Latino children learning English: Steps in the journey.* New York, NY: Teachers College Press.

ACKNOWLEDGMENTS

A partnership like Adelante cannot persist for 10-plus years without the generosity, inspiration, and hard work of many people. We can never recognize everyone by name; however, below we acknowledge many of the university and community leaders, students, activists, dedicated individuals, and the various organizations, departments, and units that have supported Adelante at different points in time.

We thank current and former University of Utah colleagues who have collaborated or offered sustained support to Adelante: Rosey Hunter, Irene Fischer, Teresa Martinez, Sarah Munro, Nate Friedman, Claire Turner, Maria Martinez, Lu Marzulli, Jennifer Lea Indo, Mario Enrique Alburges, Robin Wilks-Dunn, Juan Carlos Claudio, Jarred Martinez, Flor Olivo, Xris Martinez, Tricia Sugiyama, Feleti Matagi, Ti Kinikini, Rudy Medina, Rob Hunsaker, Joel Kincart, Adrienne Cachelin, Julie Callahan, Melanie Hooten, Joel Arvizo, Trinh Mai, David Quijada, Caitlin Cahill, Matt Bradley, Leticia Alvarez, Veronica Valdez, Mary Burbank, Audrey Thompson, Martha Bradley, Ann Darling, and Maria Fránquiz.

We also thank those community workers and educational leaders outside the university who have believed in Adelante and contributed in numerous ways: Cecilia Hernandez, Monica Gomez-Rogerson, Jessica Salazar, Robert Rendón, Archie Archuleta, Melissa Kincart, Francis Battle, Lamar Spotted Elk, Joyce Gray, Kathleen Christy, McKell Withers, and Patrick Garcia.

We thank those organizations that have provided private or public funds or in-kind resources, including Utah System of Higher Education, Eskuche Foundation, R. Harold Burton Foundation, State Farm, Herbert I. & Elsa B. Michael Foundation, George S. and Dolores Dore Eccles Foundation, Castle Foundation, Utah Hispanic Chamber of Commerce, Salt Lake City School District, Utah Coalition of La Raza, and Utah Hispanic Dance Alliance. Our University of Utah partners have been invaluable, including the Office of the President; Office of Equity and Diversity; Department of Education, Culture, & Society; Department of Educational Leadership & Policy; Office of Early Outreach; Youth Education; the Ethnic Studies Program; Center for Ethnic Student Affairs; American Indian Resource Center; the Law School's Kids' Court; MEChA; and Venceremos. A very special thank-you and acknowledgment for University Neighborhood Partners (UNP) and its leadership and staff; without their support over the years, Adelante would have never been initiated or sustained.

The college students we have worked with over the years have given their time, their hearts, and their intellect to Adelante. We offer our deep appreciation to the Adelante graduate research assistants who were the face and day-to-day coordinators of our programming: Judith Flores Carmona, Andrea Garavito Martinez, Judi Pérez-Torres, Nereida Oliva, Sylvia Mendoza, Socorro Morales, Cinthia Cervantes-Castañeda, Liliana Castrellon, Laura Zavala, Mónica Gonzalez, Anna Muñoz-Garza, and Edén Cortez. We thank the many graduate and undergraduate students who enrolled and participated in our courses, including courses such as Critical Race Theories in Education, Qualitative Methods, La Chicana, and Administration of Educational Resources. Their participation in these courses and assistance with data collection enabled us to teach, learn, and research simultaneously. We also thank the many current and former students who volunteered in different ways or were hired as camp teachers; we appreciate the ways you touched Adelante and continue to dedicate your lives to youth empowerment and community building: Pete Lelis, Nancy Huante, Cindy Hyun, Cindy Fierros, Paul Fisk, Norma Marrun, Silvia Garcia-Ibarra, Sylvia Solis, Jose Garcia, Rudy Medina, Brenda Valles, Christine Vega, Anita Juarez, Libby Atilano, Tanya Gaxiola, Ricky Gutierrez Maldonado, Ricardo Venegas, Jennyfer Morales, Daniel Cairo, Christina Endres, Enrique Soto, Annya Becerra, Rachele Jardine, Antonio De La Garza, Juan Freire, Kim Hackford-Peer, Melissa Moreno, Mohomodou Boncana, Jose Martinez, Alonso Reyna, Kehualani Folau, Brianda Galeana, Victoria (Tory) Morales, Maria Martinez, Erica Castillo, Richard Diaz, Liliana Martinez, Yamila Martinez, Lamberto Figueroa, Daniel Meza, and Ashley McKinney.

We cannot name each of the amazing undergraduate mentors who spent an hour once a week for a year at Jackson because there are approximately 700 of them who mentored between 2007 and 2015. We do, however, want them to know how grateful we are for their presence and engagement and how much impact we know they have had on the students and teachers at Jackson.

We offer a special gracias to doctoral student Liliana Castrellon, doctoral candidate Alicia De Leon, and educational leader Jana Edward. Lily has been the service learning coordinator for the Diversity Scholars Program for 5 years, and she continues to work with and coordinate all the mentors at Jackson. Alicia is carrying the Adelante torch as the Community

Learning Center coordinator at Jackson, and she currently plans and coordinates most aspects of Adelante. Jana is the principal at Jackson, and her leadership embodies the cultural affirmation, high expectations, and equity principles of Adelante.

We want to thank the scholar activists from across the country and from the spirit world (Gloria Anzaldúa and Derrick Bell) who have inspired us through their intellectual work, their writings, their activism, and, at times, their feedback. Your ideas and examples have guided our daily work and allowed us to theorize our praxis. Your names are referenced throughout the book. Thanks to Dr. James A. Banks for seeing our work as a fit with this series and to our editor Brian Ellerbeck for the depth of his patience.

We thank our respective life partners, Dr. Sonya Alemán and Dr. Octavio Villalpando. Sonya's collaboration throughout the 10 years as a parent and a scholar, creator of the Jackson newsletter, Diversity Scholar faculty coordinator, and especially as editor of our written work, helped us to shape and finish this book. Octavio's vision of creating educational pathways for students of color, his fearless commitment to the administrative transas he shared with us, and his insightful counsel have deeply influenced and helped us create the foundation of this work. Without our life partners, this work could not have been created and sustained.

Finally, and most important, we acknowledge those at Jackson—teachers, administrators and staff, parents and family members, and students. We appreciate the dedication and hard work of teachers who teach with an ethic of care and work toward culturally relevant pedagogies. We express gratitude to those administrators who have supported the college-going efforts and always prioritize the students and families. Mil gracias a los padres que sirven como ejemplos de la fuerza, perseverancia, y sabiduría para sus hijos y para nosotros. And we wish the very best for each and every Jackson student as they continue adelante on their educational journey.

INTRODUCTION

Is it true? Adelante has been canceled?

—A Jackson kindergarten parent, spring 2006

In May 2006, in the last few days of our pilot year of developing Adelante, a partnership with two dual-immersion kindergarten classrooms, we eagerly began planning our expansion into the 1st grade. Brainstorming activities for the next academic year with the two 1st-grade teachers with whom we would work during the next year, we sat in chairs designed for 6- and 7-year-olds and proceeded with planning. We shared with them our successes with our first cohort of kindergartners. The teachers appeared enthusiastic about the possibilities of having college student mentors in their classrooms and of taking field trips to the university as the kindergarten classrooms had done during the pilot year. One of the school leaders joined the meeting as we began sharing some of our preliminary findings. Gathered from the pláticas[1] (informal conversations) we had in the community room of the Day Riverside Library and in Jackson's own school library and from our initial round of data collection with kindergartners, their parents, and their college student mentors, the findings indicated overwhelmingly positive feelings about the cultivation of a college-going culture in the school and community, and of the impact that the mentoring experiences had on college students.

However, our conversations with participants also indicated other significant themes we wanted to share, especially with the two teachers who would be receiving the group of about 45 1st-grade students. Concerned about the national and state anti-immigrant and anti-Latin@[2] sentiment voiced across media outlets and debated in the state legislature, all of the participants—the children, their family members, and undergraduate mentors—shared how the current political rhetoric was strongly impacting experiences in and out of school. They viewed the anti-immigrant discourse of "being illegal" as an attack on them and their families. Parents pointed out very directly that although Adelante was promoting college

1

attendance by taking the kindergartners to the university, many key decisionmakers were communicating the exact opposite. According to these lawmakers, the parents' children did not have a right to attend school or college because of their legal residency status.

As we shared this information, the mood and tone of the meeting shifted abruptly. Engaging smiles turned to discomfort and an awkward silence fell across the room. The educational leader who had joined us interrupted and stated that this type of "debate" had nothing to do with this project. She stated plainly, "I do not want politics involved in the school." Dolores replied that sharing these data was important, given the fact that students' educational experiences were being impacted negatively. The findings could potentially help in meeting student and family concerns head-on. The educational leader replied, "I don't care about the students' legal status, and I will not let politics into this school." Enrique explained that the simple fact that Adelante and Jackson were promoting college attendance was in and of itself "political," given that the public debate focused on eliminating educational access for undocumented children. Again, the leader interrupted and firmly stated, "I don't care. We are not going to get into immigration in Adelante. If we are, then we might need to rethink the school's involvement in the program. I don't care about how they reconcile this public debate. People have been reconciling these types of issues for the 30 years I have been in education. In fact, I once had a Black principal who tried to argue the same point that I had to care about the students' culture. And it didn't work then, either!" As she progressively raised her voice, she was visibly agitated.

"How can you not care about how students in this school are being impacted by this significant debate that criminalizes who they are . . . ?" she was pointedly asked by Octavio.[3] Interrupting him before the full question could be posed, she repeated that she didn't care and that if we insisted on talking about immigration, then perhaps Adelante didn't belong in the school. Also extremely agitated, Octavio responded, "I'm shocked to hear you say you don't care. As a parent in this school, I need you to care and understand how children's educational experiences are affected by these very significant issues." He added, "And I wonder if you are a good match for this school if you don't care about something so critical to the experiences of such a large segment of this community." Then, before the leader stormed out of the classroom, she stated that she had been talking to a district administrator and he had told her, "'You can pull the plug on this program whenever you want.' So, I'm doing it now. That's it. Adelante is finished."

BUILDING ADELANTE AS A
UNIVERSITY–SCHOOL–COMMUNITY PARTNERSHIP

From the beginning, Adelante was conceived as a university–school–community partnership specifically constructed as a pathway toward higher education, for Chican@Latin@[4] and other students of color, first-generation students, immigrant children, and those who have been historically underrepresented in higher education. We–the founders of the partnership–asked ourselves, "What would it look like if a school began to cultivate college awareness and expectations starting with 5-year-olds? How could we as university faculty and parents of children in this school utilize our connections to the benefit of the students and families in this community that we were a part of?" We firmly believed the underlying goals would be viewed as benign, a "no-brainer," a perspective with which all possible stakeholders would be in agreement. And as we initiated our engagement with the first cohort of kindergartners–L@s Primer@s–our process of getting to know parents and students, and of understanding their concerns, we heard about the stark realities impacting their lives. We sought to share these experiences, concerns, and challenges with the school, so that we could all learn from and develop alternative ways for creating and nurturing additive educative spaces.

Now, well over a decade after it transpired, the last meeting of the pilot year described above continues to remind us of how resistant dominant perspectives can be and how entrenched majoritarian deficit notions remain in many schools serving students of color or, more specifically, Chican@Latin@ students. For the educational leader who boldly stated that she would end the partnership, her threat never materialized. Yet, her response illustrates how affirming the challenges of Chican@Latin@ students' daily lives, taking them to the university, or shifting a school's culture to one that emphasizes college expectations can be radical and threatening to some educators.

As Chican@ parents, scholars, educators, and activists, we understand the (mis)education of Chican@Latin@ students in U.S. public and higher education contexts to be historically evident, directly linked to racialized policies and systems, and deeply rooted in deficit-oriented educational practices (Acuña, 1988; Delgado Bernal, 1999; Donato, 1997; San Miguel & Valencia, 1998; Solórzano & Yosso, 2001a; Valencia, 2008; Yosso, 2006). In schools that serve majority Chican@Latin@ student populations–and in those that serve other students of color, for that matter–educational programs are all too often underresourced (Alemán, 2007; Biddle & Berliner, 2002; Brady, Eatman, & Parker, 2000; Carey, 2004; Kozol, 1991, 2012), fail to promote a college-going culture (Auerbach, 2002; Jarsky, McDonough, & Núñez, 2009), and do not capitalize on the richness of home and community knowledges as culturally relevant assets in their curricula and pedagogical strategies (Delgado Bernal, 2002; Gonzalez et al., 1995; Guajardo, Guajardo, & Del Carmen Casaperalta, 2008). Utilizing critical race and Chicana feminist theories to critique and amend the manner by which educational opportunity has been parceled out to some and denied to others (Alemán, 2006, 2007; Delgado Bernal, 1999; Delgado Bernal & Villalpando, 2002), we are abundantly aware that public schools in the United States have been designed to work against the vast majority of Chican@Latin@ students and communities.

In K–12 settings particularly, scholars have traced historical neglect (Delgado Bernal, 1999; San Miguel & Valencia, 1998), described litigation that has spurred incremental reform (Valencia, 2008), and charted social and educational policies that have systematically disadvantaged and oppressed Chican@Latin@ students, parents, and communities (Gándara & Contreras, 2009). Some have also documented how state legislative reform has been influenced by private interests (Valenzuela, 2004), whereas others have critiqued the racial hierarchies that are often implemented at the district level (Alemán, 2007). In regard to higher education, Chican@Latin@ students are sorely underrepresented on university campuses, and many of the few who overcome K–12 educational barriers are tracked into community colleges with limited chances to transfer to 4-year institutions (Villalpando, 2010). Some scholars have also demonstrated that the school-to-prison pipeline, particularly for Chicano and Latino males, is more solidified than the school-to-college pipeline (Valles & Villalpando, 2013). So, although we fully recognize and unequivocally declare that pervasive and comprehensive educational inequity and systemic oppression has had cumulative effects on Chican@Latin@ students and communities, we do not wish to belabor the point in this book. Our colleagues have spoken to these issues in other seminal works (Gándara & Contreras, 2009; Pizarro, 2005; Valencia, 2008; Valenzuela, 1999; Yosso, 2006). Rather, we present our work with a university–school–community partnership as one way of disrupting and destabilizing the ubiquitous coloniality, racism, and unequal educational opportunities in the nation's schools and educational systems.

Therefore, this book is about the first decade (2005–2015) of our ongoing journey of developing and sustaining a university–school–community partnership designed to challenge and counter the educational system's failure to educate Chican@Latin@ students in our community. It is not a how-to book that provides a simplistic step-by-step model or one-size-fits-all prescription for creating a university–school–community partnership, though it does provide important insights into this process. Instead,

this book chronicles a messy theoretical and practical journey and offers
consejos (advice) to those interested in disrupting the (mis)education of
Chican@sLatin@s. We present the barriers, mistakes, and tensions we experienced in confronting institutional racism and describe the ways that resilience can challenge colonial legacies of educational inequity that deny
equal educational opportunity and academic success for Chican@Latin@
students (Gándara & Contreras, 2009; Pizarro, 2005; Urrieta, 2009). We
share the challenges of sustaining, for the first 10 years, a university–school–
community partnership in an underresourced school located in one of the
most politically conservative states in the United States, and we demonstrate how we centered marginalized knowledges and supported the cultural
affirmation of Chican@Latin@ students while attempting to influence the
school's culture. Buttressed by a range of campus and community partners,
we document the hope and desire expressed by Spanish-speaking parents
who want equal educational opportunities for their children, by bilingual
elementary school students who say they want to go to college, by undergraduate students of color who mentor Chican@Latin@ youth, by teachers
who want to improve their practice, and by a community that has been
educationally marginalized for too long. We hope that educators, activists,
and educational researchers who read this book gain insight into the work
involved in developing and sustaining purposeful and authentic university–
school–community partnerships that are intentionally designed to serve the
interests and disrupt the (mis)education of Chican@Latin@ students specifically, and students of color more generally.

The purpose of this book, therefore, is threefold and is grounded in
both practical and theoretical contributions. First, we discuss our partnership work—its development, implementation, and sustainability—and its
potential for inciting transformative ruptures for Chican@Latin@ students
and communities within a colonial racial realist framework. We conceptualize transformative ruptures as those incidents, interactions, experiences,
and moments that expose and interrupt pervasive coloniality and structural
inequities. Transformative ruptures allow us to put theory into practice by
acknowledging the sustained creation of small, but significant, anticolonial[5]
shifts in inequitable practices, discourses, and policies. Within the fissures
of oppressive structures there is an understanding that transformative ruptures can multiply and offer opportunities for change and possibility. Thus,
this university–school–community partnership was crafted in the pursuit of
transformative ruptures to the (mis)education of Chican@Latin@ students.

Second, we seek to recast university–school–community partnerships as
reciprocal, subversive, and enduring projects. Too often, university partnerships are conceptualized as hierarchical relationships, with university leaders

and scholars from outside of the community having the knowledge and expertise needed to "save" communities of color or "train" school district and school-based leaders (Benson & Harkavy, 2001; Benson, Harkavy, & Puckett, 2007). These partnerships rarely attempt to destabilize racist structures while prioritizing the needs of marginalized communities, nor do they infuse equity and social justice work in sustainable and comprehensive ways. We attempt to fill this void by pointing to the micropolitical maneuvering involved in doing partnership work within a racialized, gendered, and colonial landscape. In doing so, we give examples of those strategies and practices we employed as Chican@ activist scholars working from within multiple educational institutions in order to destabilize the inequity within those institutions.

And finally, we lay out the challenges and successes of doing this work, of cultivating transformative ruptures, by proposing a critical race feminista praxis—an anticolonial approach that embodies the goals of advocacy scholarship and fuses the tenets of critical race theories[6] (Lynn & Dixson, 2013; D. G. Solórzano, 1998; Yosso, 2006) with the analytical tools of Anzaldúan Chicana feminist theories (Anzaldúa, 1987, 2000, 2005; Elenes, 2011; Keating, 2006). Outlining the theoretical contours of this praxis in Chapter 2, we provide examples of what it looks like in practice throughout the book.

We take seriously the challenges posed to those in academia, and to those seeking to "work at the intersection of multiple theoretical and methodological approaches that coalesce in our work on the ground in/with communities . . ." (Stovall, 2016, pp. 385–386). Almost 20 years ago, Gloria Ladson-Billings (1998) warned that critical race theory in education might continue to generate scholarly papers and debate, but she doubted it would ever be seriously engaged in K–12 classrooms and in the daily education of students of color. Today, both critical race and Chicana feminist scholarship continue to be grounded in theory and analysis with few examples of what these theories can look like in practice, especially in public K–12 education.[7] This book, therefore, contributes to the ongoing scholarly and practical discussions of Chican@Latin@ student success by pushing forward a real-world application of critical race feminista praxis. Together, these three purposes help us document our journey in developing and sustaining Adelante.

AN OVERVIEW OF WHAT FOLLOWS

We have organized the book into six chapters. The first chapter introduces the research via our positionalities as activist scholars and parents of school-age children who participated in the partnership. Describing how the university–school–community partnership was initiated in 2005, we set the Utah and Salt Lake City context as unique because of the dominant religious influence and as familiar because of the inequitable schooling that is provided to Chican@Latin@ students. The chapter ends with an introduction to the neighborhood and Jackson Elementary as sites where the partnership was founded and developed.

Chapter 2 delineates our use of the metaphor of a trenza (braid) in describing the theoretical strands we weave together for our critical race feminista praxis. Explaining key ideas and concepts, we point to how our work is anticolonial and draws from both critical race theory and Chicana feminist theories. We offer transformative ruptures as an amalgamation of these theories and as one way to make meaning of our praxis that attempts to destabilize indestructible structures of inequity. We also introduce the idea of transas (transactions/strategies) (Urrieta, 2009) as one way to understand the daily tactics and practices we employed to develop and sustain the Adelante partnership.

Chapter 3 describes how the original cohort of Adelante kindergartners, now in their junior year in high school, experienced the partnership activities. In recounting their participation in different aspects of Adelante, they share how they related to their college mentors, what they learned from the Oral History Project, and how they were impacted by the numerous university field trips and the overall exposure they had to higher education during elementary school. The chapter ends with a look at some of the positive academic outcomes of L@s Primer@s, as well as the pattern of academic exclusion.

Chapter 4 centers on the roles that parents, teachers, and administrators played in the school as well as some of their relationships with one another and the partnership. After highlighting the engagement and leadership of parents, the chapter addresses some of the choques (collisions) (Anzaldúa, 1987) present at Jackson. One persistent choque was between the deficit-based discourses in the school and the asset-based principles of Adelante. We believe this omnipresent choque provides the backdrop for many of the fractures that have been present at Jackson. We describe one choque between the parents and school staff because it exemplifies nepantla, or a liminal space that was full of angst, discomfort, and conflict, as well as ripe with potential for transformative ruptures to emerge. The chapter concludes by sharing the bridge building that was necessary after the said choque.

In Chapter 5, we focus on the mentoring component of Adelante. The first half of the chapter documents the transas used to create and develop the Diversity Scholars Program, a first-year academic support and retention program that provides freshmen student-of-color mentors to Adelante.

We argue that the Diversity Scholars Program illustrates a transformative rupture to a predominantly White institution (PWI). The second half of the chapter turns to how the mentors make sense of their experiences mentoring at Jackson and participating in the Diversity Scholars Program. We use Gloria Anzaldúa's conceptualization of nepantla to make sense of how college students of color reflect on the ongoing construction of their identities and the learning they engage via their mentoring and participation in the Diversity Scholars Program.

In the last chapter, we provide consejos for engaging in critical race feminista praxis. Our consejos are organized around three interconnected and overlapping concepts that we introduce and discuss in Chapters 1 through 5: nepantla, transas, and transformative ruptures. These three ideas help us organize theoretical, methodological, and practical consejos for activist scholars/educators interested in working from within educational institutions. We describe some of the different types of transas we employed to coordinate, fund, grow, and sustain Adelante. We end with a discussion of the importance of finding "success" in individual, structural, and collective transformative ruptures.

CHAPTER ONE

THE ORIGIN AND CONTEXT
OF ADELANTE

We begin by sharing some of who we are and how we began Adelante in order to be transparent about the biases and motivations we bring to the partnership work. Because we know that research and knowledge production is closely linked to the subjectivities of a researcher (Delgado Bernal, 1998; Rusell y Rodríguez, 1998), we realize that this book is as much about Chican@Latin@ education and partnership work as it is about our own journeys. One of our mentors once said, "research is me-search," meaning research often seeks to understand our experiences, our realities, and ourselves. We both know that our personal, professional, and communal identities are closely linked to the partnership work we have done (Delgado Bernal, 2008). It is also clear to us that all of our identities—as parents of school-age children, as a Chicana and Chicano educator, as first-generation college students but fourth- and fifth-generation Mexican Americans, as individuals with limited Spanish-speaking proficiency, as products of K–12 public schooling, and as activist scholars—inform how and why we initiated Adelante.

We both brought with us years of experiences, perspectives, and mistakes working in different realms of educational research, policy, and practice. I (Dolores) started working in Chican@Latin@ education in Kansas City, Missouri, in 1986 with Guadalupe Center Inc., first as a summer day-camp director and parent involvement coordinator, and then as the director of a bilingual preschool. After moving to California, I worked as an educational specialist with National Council of La Raza (NCLR), a public elementary school teacher in Pasadena Unified School District, a teacher educator at UCLA, and also a student, teacher, and researcher in the fields of Chican@ studies and education. I (Enrique) was engaged with policy work early in my career, working at the local, state, and federal levels before beginning my academic appointment. Oddly enough, one of my first positions was as an intern and then as a full-time staffer for the Central Intelligence Agency. In leaving the agency and returning to Texas, I worked on issues more directly aligned to my values—school finance equity, educational leadership for empowerment, and community transformation—and in pre-dominantly Chican@ communities in South Texas.

Key to the origin story of Adelante is the story of our lives as parents. My (Dolores's) husband, Dr. Octavio Villalpando, and I have three children who were 1, 3, and 5 years old when Adelante kicked off in 2005. We arrived in Salt Lake City from Monterey, California, in 1999, both of us accepting tenure-track faculty positions at the University of Utah in the College of Education. My joint appointment was in a department soon to be renamed the Department of Education, Culture, and Society and in the Ethnic Studies Program. Arriving childless, we moved to the city's trendy and less ethnically diverse Eastside neighborhood situated close to the university, where we anticipated it would be easy to sell our home when, in a short time, we would move on to our next faculty gig. Four years later, expecting our third child and with our oldest son less than a year away from starting kindergarten, we made a conscious choice to move to one of the city's ethnically diverse Westside communities. Octavio and I did not want our boys growing up facing constant microaggressions or paying for their "good" Eastside education with experiences of isolation, alienation, rootless-ness, or denial of their identities. Wanting to avoid what Beverly Daniel Tatum (1999) calls the "assimilation blues," we instead chose to live on the Westside, and to send our sons to a Westside school.

My (Enrique's) wife, Dr. Sonya M. Alemán, and I have three children who were 1, 5, and 9 years old when we initiated Adelante. We arrived in Salt Lake City from Austin, Texas, in 2004, when I accepted my first position in the academy as an assistant professor in the Department of Educational Leadership and Policy at the University of Utah. Similarly, Sonya and I chose to live in the same Westside neighborhood of Salt Lake City as Dolores and Octavio so that our children could grow up and go to school around families of color. Moving from Texas, our primary concern was raising our Chican@ children in a predominantly White, conservative, and religious state. We were aware that the schools would expose our children to cultural norms that were not congruent with our values, and we were concerned with the less-than-rigorous educational experiences they would have in the public schools. We wanted them to be in a community that felt more like home, but we also recognized the long history of inferior schooling to which students on the Westside were often exposed.

So although both of our families chose to reside in a working-class community of color and send our children to Jackson Elementary[1]—the site of our future partnership—this decision was not always an easy one because living and going to school in working-class communities of color typically translates into underresourced schools, fewer educational opportunities, and lower teacher expectations (Kozol, 2012; Oakes, 1985; Valenzuela, 1999).

As educational researchers and as parents of Brown children,[2] we knew this. So, we thought the time opportune to develop a partnership between the University of Utah and Jackson when a university call for proposals was released encouraging submissions for partnerships seeking to raise awareness of higher education opportunities in Salt Lake City's Westside communities.[3] We also thought this would allow us to apply our scholarly expertise, tap into our professional networks, and replicate for all students some of the educational opportunities and high academic expectations to which our children would have been exposed if they were attending schools on the predominantly White Eastside of the city.

use privilege to average [handwritten marginal note]

It was in the spring of 2005, while we were sitting in one of the meeting rooms of a public library on the Westside of Salt Lake, trying to meet the grant proposal deadline with Octavio and recently arrived doctoral student Judith Flores Carmona, that the name for our proposed partnership—"Adelante: A College Awareness and Preparatory Partnership"—was agreed upon. Adelante translates to "forward," "forward moving," or "looking forward," and we began to conceptualize it that day as a university–school–community partnership that seeks to raise awareness of higher education opportunities and to increase the expectation of future university attendance and success among students, families, and teachers at Jackson. Adelante is premised on the simple, yet radical, belief (for some) that all young people, including young people of color, should be expected and prepared to enroll and succeed in college, and that college preparation must emphasize students' intellectual development in relation to their racial and cultural identities and their community. The partnership's main objectives are to (1) prepare students and their families for college by integrating higher education into their school experience, and (2) help establish a college-going culture within the school. Although the partnership's primary focus is to build college awareness and raise expectations of higher education attendance and success among elementary students, the fact that we work with teachers, parents, university students (in their capacity as undergraduate mentors and graduate research assistants), and community partners provides an opportunity for the effects of the partnership to be far-reaching.

Shortly after the meeting in the library, we met with an educational leader at Jackson Elementary and shared the grant possibility. We condensed our idea of constructing a college-going atmosphere in a school to the benign notion of taking elementary youth as young as kindergarten age to the university on field trips, and of bringing the university to the school in the form of undergraduate mentors of color. Because of the simplicity of our suggestion, we reasoned that it would be difficult to reject. We were taken aback by the educational leader's very first response to our proposal:

Why not take the kids to the park down the street? They won't know the difference and it will solve the issues that will come up in regard to scheduling the school buses. And these parents? I don't know how many you will actually get involved. My Hispanic parent involvement at this school is pretty low. They don't value it. I can't get anyone here on a Family Math Night even though I offer to feed them.

As parents of children who were about to start kindergarten in the school and as university faculty members who wanted to utilize our university contacts for the benefit of the school, we were disappointed. As scholars who engage and utilize the guiding principles of critical race theory, however, we were not surprised, situating the response within the deficit-laden discourses that often describe Chican@Latin@ students and families. After all, we were living and doing our work in a state where fiscally and socially conservative leaders dominate the political landscape. We were operating within a context where fear and jingoistic, anti-Latin@ sentiment seemed to fan across the national public airwaves on a daily basis. In spite of that first meeting with one school leader, the partnership began shortly thereafter. Building relationships with families and teachers, engaging with youth in our first year, and beginning the planning for the second year, we pushed forward in developing our programs. Yet, that deeply troubling statement from a school leader continued to represent itself in multiple forms throughout the school, challenging our abilities to operate cohesively and in mutually beneficial ways. This prevalent deficit perspective would gnaw at the core of the partnership's guiding framework throughout our first 10 years.

RESEARCH AS INTERVENTION

Our research can be categorized as community-engaged scholarship, action research, or more appropriately, anticolonial research. We say much more about the theory and methodology that guide our research in the next chapter, but what is important to note here is that we initiated this research as an intervention into the failing educational processes for Chican@Latin@ students in an underfunded urban school, rather than as an academic study disconnected from the material realities of a predominantly Brown community. We wanted to utilize our privileges as university professors to advocate for the best education possible for our children, as well as for the youth in our working-class community. We do not mean to suggest that our research plan was not well conceived. Indeed, we addressed the partnership's broader implications in the Internal Review Board (IRB) application since the first year of the partnership, consulted and collaborated with school district data and assessment administrators, presented our research at national conferences, and have published more than a dozen articles and chapters. However, in reflecting back over the years, it is unmistakable that even though we were aware that the partnership would generate knowledge that could possibly impact the educational practices affecting Chican@Latin@ students, our immediate priority was often focused on impacting day-to-day practice and policy at this one particular school. In other words, there were many times that the programmatic needs (for example, making sure that a bus was scheduled for a field trip to the university, that undergraduate mentors had carpools set up to get to the school, or that food was ordered for the teachers' professional development), took precedence over data collection, data analysis, and writing.

Nonetheless, our partnership was equally a longitudinal study, originally guided by five main themes of inquiry: (1) the college-going culture of Jackson Elementary; (2) the change in awareness of higher education among students and parents; (3) the extent to which the university–school–community partnership affects student achievement; (4) the manner by which mentoring relationships influence (elementary and university) student experiences; and (5) the ways in which the cultural component of the partnership impacts students, parents, and teachers. In the tradition of qualitative research (Denzin & Lincoln, 2005), other questions and topics of inquiry emerged, such as parents' cultural citizenship (Delgado Bernal, Alemán, & Flores Carmona, 2008), parent and family engagement and leadership (Alemán, Pérez-Torres, & Oliva, 2013; Boncana, 2010), culturally relevant teacher pedagogies (Freire, 2014), student experiences in an after-school Chican@ studies class (Mendoza, 2014, 2015; Morales, 2016), undergraduate mentoring experiences (Delgado Bernal, Alemán, & Garavito, 2009), and pedagogies of Latina immigrant mothers (Flores Carmona, 2010; Flores Carmona, & Delgado Bernal, 2012). We have been able to address multiple themes of inquiry and simultaneously chronicle the ongoing journey of a university–school–community partnership via a wealth of data collected over the years.

We collected data from 2005 to 2015 in collaboration with numerous graduate students, almost exclusively Chican@, who have worked with us as research assistants, as well as with other students enrolled in our courses that provided research experience with the partnership (for example, Critical Race Theories in Education, Qualitative Methods, La Chicana, Administration of Educational Resources). The data we drew upon to write this book come primarily from 10 years of participant observations; individual and group pláticas (Fierros & Delgado Bernal, 2016) with elementary school students, parents, teachers, and college student mentors; a schoolwide parent questionnaire in 2010; a teacher survey in the fall of 2011; and achievement data from the district. Since 2005, more than 160 interviews have been audiotaped, with some videotaped. Our students transcribed the interviews, and with guidance, we often asked them to conduct the first phase of data analysis. Our baseline data from 2005 included our first interviews with the pilot group of kindergartners, L@s Primer@s. Focusing on six simple inquiries, we asked questions such as (1) Do you know what college is? (2) Have you ever visited a college? and (3) Do you know anybody who goes to college? Over the years we have interviewed L@s Primer@s four times.

What has made this research on educational pathways to higher education exciting and difficult is its longitudinal nature. Though actual college attendance is not the only measure of success for a university–school–community partnership focused on college awareness, it is certainly an important one. We knew when we initiated Adelante that we would not know how many of the original students would go on to college until 13 years after they started kindergarten at Jackson. Coupled with the mobility of poor, working-class, and many immigrant families, this time frame has indeed been a challenge. We started off with 47 kindergartners. By the beginning of 2nd grade, some had moved away and others had joined the class, for a total of 37 students—22 girls and 15 boys. Today, we know where 30 of those original 47 students are, and of those 30, only 17 attended the middle school that Jackson students feed into. Chapter 3 specifically focuses on L@s Primer@s; however, throughout the book we explore the partnership more holistically to include the school culture, the nearly 1,500 students who have participated in Adelante, their parents and families, Jackson teachers and school leaders, and the nearly 700 university student mentors.

The graduate student research assistants who have worked with Adelante have been the face and the backbone of the partnership. Since 2005, we have hired and prepared one Chicano and 12 Chicana full-time graduate assistants, all of whom are bilingual with different levels of Spanish literacy, come from working-class families, and are mostly first-generation college students.[4] Recognizing their contributions as activist scholars, they are[5] Judith Flores Carmona, Andrea Garavito Martinez, Estela Hernandez, Judi Pérez-Torres, Nereida Oliva, Sylvia Mendoza, Socorro Morales, Cinthia Cervantes-Castañeda, Liliana Castrellon, Laura Zavala, Mónica Gonzalez, Anna Muñoz-Garza, and Edén Cortez. These individuals have been key liaisons with parents, elementary students, college student mentors, and teachers, and their leadership in implementing programmatic and research activities has been crucial to the partnership. They have presented their research with Adelante at education and/or Chican@ studies conferences.

Six of our former students—Judith Flores Carmona, Mohomodou Boncana, Juan Freire, Sylvia Mendoza, Socorro Morales, and Jana Edward—have completed their dissertations on different aspects of Adelante, and two additional graduate students—Judith Pérez-Torres and Neri Oliva—are in the final stages of writing up their findings, one based on her work with Adelante mothers and the other based on her work with mentors. Perhaps most important to us and to the partnership work is that each of the graduate research assistants created genuine relationships with different partnership participants, especially with students, parents, and families. These relationships have fostered political and methodological collaboration (Foley & Valenzuela, 2008), spaces of convivencia (living together in community) from which to form solidarity for school change (Dyrness, 2008), and reciprocal exchanges that build confianza (trust) between participants and researchers. We address the importance and difficulties of graduate student training for activist scholars in Chapter 6. However, here we emphasize that the relationships these activist scholars, who carry a colonizer/colonized identity (Villenas, 1996), forged with parents, students, and teachers were crucial not only to the partnership work, but also to our research design and process.

THE UTAH CONTEXT AS DISTINCT AND ALL TOO FAMILIAR

Our work with Adelante is located in a Utah context that is unique and simultaneously similar to that of other states. The context is unique because Utah state politics and culture are dominated by the predominant Mormon faith and the area is a bastion of conservative thought and practice (Alemán & Rorrer, 2006; Bulkeley, 2005, 2008; Davis & Archer, 2005; Lynn, 2005; Sanchez, 2007, 2008; Sanchez & Lyon, 2006; A. Solórzano, 1998, 2005, 2006). Salt Lake City is the international headquarters for the Church of Jesus Christ of Latter-day Saints (LDS) and remains the center of LDS culture, politics, leadership, and policy. Because of the church's influence on state policy, it often seems that Thomas Jefferson's interpretation of "separation of church and state" is nonexistent in Utah. Simultaneously, the state's context is similar to that in other states that have experienced a diversifying population since the 1990s (Perlich, 2002, 2004, 2008) and have failed to provide equal educational access and opportunities to Chican@Latin@ students (Alemán & Rorrer, 2006). As a result of Utah's over-a-decade-long pattern of immigration, the state has benefited from younger workers and the low-wage, semi-skilled abilities that immigrant communities bring. As documented by Pam Perlich (2004, 2008), senior economist with the University of Utah's Bureau of Economic Analysis, the state has reaped the social and economic benefits of these migrants, who come predominantly from Mexico. Perlich (2004) states,

> In the absence of immigration, Utah would have experienced labor shortages, bottlenecks, higher costs, and reduction in economic activity. In fact, according to the Bureau of the Census, Utah would have experienced a net out-migration from the state for at least the last five years had it not been for the continued arrival of immigrants. (p. 13)

Perlich further contends that "not only have these immigrants contributed to the demographic growth, relative youth, and diversity of the state, they have provided labor that was vital to the economic boom of the 1990s and the successful hosting of the Winter Olympic Games" (p. 14).

An element of the narrative of Utah's growing immigrant communities is the passing of conflicting legislation that negatively impacts these economically, politically, and socially vulnerable communities. For example, in 2011 Utah passed the Illegal Immigration Enforcement Act (HB 497), also referred to as the "show me your papers law." It was a far-reaching enforcement-only bill that copied several provisions virtually outright from Arizona's controversial Support Our Law Enforcement and Safe Neighborhoods Act (SB 1070), a bill known as one of the broadest and strictest anti-immigrant laws across the nation. Although Utah's law was not quite as extreme or draconian, both laws gave local police officers unconstitutional authority to suspect the citizenship and immigration status of anyone they stopped for allegedly committing any crime, including jaywalking or minor traffic offenses.[6] Seemingly contradictory is the passing, nearly a decade earlier, of the Exemption from Nonresident Tuition state law (HB 144) that offers in-state tuition to undocumented students. Though there have been strong efforts to repeal HB 144 since it passed in 2002, Utah remains one of 16 states that allows undocumented students who meet specific eligibility requirements to pay in-state tuition. Interestingly, the conservative LDS church and its focus on "family values" has influenced the passing of these and other anti-immigrant and pro-immigrant laws in Utah.

Also central to the sociopolitical climate of the partnership is the state of education in Utah. Based on reports from the U.S. Census Bureau, Utah has been ranked dead last in per-pupil spending over the past several years and has historically ranked among the worst-funded public school systems in the country.[7] In the context of this low spending, the state of Utah continues to fall short at providing equal educational access and opportunities for students of color, and Chican@Latin@ students in particular (Alemán & Rorrer, 2006; Sanderson, 2005). Latin@s now make up 12% of the total state population and 14.4% of the K–12 student population. In the Salt Lake City School District (SLCD)–the district in which the partnership is located–40% of the total student enrollment is Latin@. One of the largest and most diverse districts in the state, SLCD provides a window into the future of Utah's public school student population.

Exhibiting segregation along geographic lines, Eastside schools in SLCD are disproportionately White and have the largest number of students categorized as high socioeconomic status. Westside schools, where Jackson is located, are mostly made up of students of color and families that are disproportionately classified as low socioeconomic status. In regard to access to rigorous and specialized academic programming, magnet programs and those developed as college-preparatory programs are mostly located in Eastside schools. The only program not located in an Eastside school–the district's high school International Baccalaureate (IB) program–is located three blocks from Jackson in a school that is 60% students of color and 42% Latin@. Despite being located in this racially diverse school, 73% of students in the IB program are identified as White and only 8% are Latin@. Though racial segregation and inaccessibility to specialized, enrichment, or college-preparatory curriculum is a specific backdrop to our partnership work, we reiterate that this in-school segregation is also quite common to urban settings throughout the country.

Also important to the sociopolitical climate of the partnership is the fact that the University of Utah, the state's flagship university, is located in Salt Lake City's Eastside, about 4 miles from Jackson Elementary. Nestled along the foothills of the Wasatch Mountains, views of the Salt Lake Valley and Great Salt Lake are spectacular. Induction into the Pacific 12 (Pac 12) conference, modern light rail and student housing–both constructed during the buildup to the 2002 Winter Olympics–and updated academic facilities, including new buildings for the Schools of Law, Education, Business, and Dentistry, are signs of a university in forward motion. Yet, despite outward appearances and several public initiatives that at first glance appear to promote inclusion and the further diversification of the campus, the institution, similar to other predominantly White universities, has often silenced diverse perspectives and fomented an overtly hostile racial campus climate toward first-generation students of color. For example, among all major universities, the University of Utah remains one of the select few in maintaining a Native American athletics logo and team "mascot." Whether during one of the "Runnin' Utes" basketball games during the NCAA March Madness tournament or an ESPN Thursday Night football telecast of a football game, countless images of undergraduates in Native "headdresses" or in "red face" are commonly viewed across the nation. These images are connected to the Drum and Feather logo that is sanctioned by the institution.[8]

A PORTRAIT OF THE NEIGHBORHOOD AND THE SCHOOL

Although it is only 4 miles from the community in which they live and go to school, the university has for many years been inaccessible to many families at Jackson. Located in the Guadalupe neighborhood, Jackson Elementary also serves the Rose Park and Fairgrounds neighborhoods. Sandwiched between a peach-colored building that reads "Church of Tonga" on one side and a major freeway on the other, the school was first built in the late 1800s and last rebuilt in the early 1980s. A short walk from school, a block away, is a large Latin@ food market where many Jackson parents and families do their grocery shopping. Also within short walking distance are several fast-food restaurants like Pizza Hut and McDonald's, along with local, family-owned eating establishments such as Beto's and El Asadero. Running in front of these restaurants is the city's light rail system, with a stop that shares the Jackson name. The Jackson stop is adorned with amazingly colorful artwork by Ruby Chacon, a Salt Lake City Chicana artist, whose work can be found throughout the city (and on this book's cover), along with the written poetry of youth and local poets. Around this rail stop, in the evenings especially, is evidence of prostitution. Catty-corner from the Jackson stop is a more upscale Mexican food restaurant, popular among many White Utahans who are not from the local neighborhood. It is not unusual to see patrons waiting for their table to be ready, huddling together for warmth on the sidewalks adjacent to its front door during the Utah winter months.

Located on the same block as Jackson, but on the backside of the school is the Guadalupe Catholic Church that many Jackson students and their families attend. The east side of this church faces the freeway and an underpass for street traffic. Inside the underpass is a large mosaic mural representing the diversity of the community with Navajo code talkers, a flamenco dancer, a doctor, a lawyer, a farmer, and Pacific Islander dancers. Another local Chicano artist worked with other community artists, community members, and especially youth to design and create the mural. A resident and activist in this community, his artwork and creativity capture the beauty, diversity, and strength of the community.

The residential area surrounding Jackson is similar to what might be seen in other low-income neighborhoods in mid-sized cities. There is a house that is located directly across from the Tongan Church that many students reference as "abandoned and haunted." This house appears to not have had occupants in many years; it has a yellowed and dirt-filled grassy area on both sides, and wooden boards cover its windows. According to some students who attend Jackson, houses like this one, abandoned and unattended, can be found throughout their neighborhood. The houses located near and around Jackson are single-family homes and apartment complexes, usually with older cars parked on the street or in driveways. Though there are only two small parks within walking distance of Jackson, not far away there is a large, fairly new county recreational center that offers a range of sporting activities and exercise classes for youth and adults. If you walk through the neighborhood on school days in the morning or afternoon, it is common to see mothers, fathers, grandparents, or other adults walking with children to school or watching children cross at one of the crosswalks.

Jackson Elementary, a neighborhood school, provides a dual-language immersion program to anyone from within the school boundary wishing to enroll their child and accepts transfers from families from outside the boundary, but within the school district. Unlike the only other dual-immersion program in the district (which is located in an Eastside school), Jackson does not have the resources or district approval to operate its dual-immersion program as a specialized or application-only program for students deemed qualified for admittance. The student makeup of those in the regular track program and those in the immersion program are somewhat similar along racial and socioeconomic lines. According to the 2012 fall school enrollment report by the Utah State Office of Education (USOE), there were 327 "Hispanic" students enrolled out of a total of 459 students, which is 71.2% of the school population (Utah State Office of Education, 2012). The overwhelming majority of students, 85%, qualified for free or reduced-price lunch during the 2012–2013 academic year (Utah State Office of Education, 2012). School-level data shared by district officials and school administration indicate that close to half (47.5%) of the students are classified as English language learners. However, similar to most urban schools with a racially/ ethnically diverse student population, the demographics of the teaching force do not mirror the student population. In 2011, 92% of the school's faculty self-identified as White and 96% identified as female. There were 24 classroom teachers, nine of them teaching in the dual-language immersion program. These data remained consistent during the ten years we developed the partnership.

Jackson Elementary has changed both its outward and inward appearance during the 10 years we write about. In the initial years of Adelante, the school itself contained almost no visual markers that made it distinct from any other Title I school in the area or that pointed to a college-going culture. Originally constructed in 1892, the current building was built from the ground up in 1983 and the outside of the building was painted a tan-brown color with a chain-link fence encompassing the playground area and school grounds. The interior school walls were dingy white, with no color in the hallways other than student artwork boards scattered between classrooms. The inside of Jackson is somewhat U-shaped, with two long hallways that are connected in some parts by smaller hallways. Tan lockers are spread throughout both sides of these hallways. The drabness of the school itself made the school look and feel unwelcoming.

The look and feel of Jackson in 2015 is very different from how it was in the early years of the partnership. Upon approaching the school, the previously plain chain-link fence now contains the phrase "Jackson Cougars, where children roar and families soar" in both English and Spanish. The two large pillars right before the main entrance of Jackson, once plain white, now greet those who enter with bright and colorful permanent artwork. A banner reading "Jackson Elementary: Home of future college students/Hogar de futuros estudiantes universitarios" hangs at the front of the building next to the kindergarten classrooms, communicating the school's emphasis on college awareness. In partnership with university students, Jackson established a community garden in 2011 that today brings community members together to plant, water, and harvest a healthy garden of flowers and vegetables.

The vibrancy of the recently painted green, red, purple, and orange walls and white trim now accent the interior foyer and main hallways of the school. The walls speak words of inspiration with large block-lettered quotes by the likes of Malcolm X, the Dalai Lama, Maya Angelou, and Isabel Allende. Below an exit sign and framing the top of one hallway are the words "¡Adelante-Arriba-Siempre!" There are also wooden squares of artwork located on the top of the walls above the lockers with college logos from schools such as the University of Texas at Austin and the University of Utah. On one wing of the U-shape, there is student mural representing a map of the neighborhood created by a class of 3rd-graders. All of these changes have significantly impacted the atmosphere, contributing to a college-going culture and a more welcoming environment that can inspire.

In this chapter, we sketched out the context for the partnership's setting, including our positionality and motivation as scholar activists, the school community and neighborhoods we engage, and the facilities and resources we rely on to situate our programs and research. Now, we turn our attention to a discussion of the critical race and Chicana feminist theoretical frameworks that inform both the partnership's goals and programs, as well as our research design, approach, and objectives.

CHAPTER TWO

TRENZA IN OUR PARTNERSHIP WORK

The trenza is an Indigenous hairstyle that continues to be worn by both women and men. There are numerous teachings and meanings about the trenza, but to American Indian and Mexican Indian persons, and in Chican@ history, it has significant cultural meanings. Some of the first acts of colonialism in the Americas were to strip away language, deny history and religion, and cut Indigenous people's hair. Therefore, reclaiming the trenza, practically or metaphorically, may be thought of as an anticolonial act. Over the years, a number of Chicana scholars have used the trenza as a metaphor to make theoretical connections to phenomena that are encoded with cultural meaning. For example, critical race legal scholar Margaret Montoya (1994) speaks of conceptual trenzas as the re-braided ideas of our multicultural lives, which provide opportunities for unmasking the subordinating effects of academic discourse. Francisca González (1998) speaks of the trenzas of multiple identities, as well as trenzas as the analytical tool that helps her braid together multiple theoretical frames.

We utilize the trenza metaphor in two ways. First, the metaphor refers to our critical race feminista praxis—an anticolonial praxis that braids together critical race theories (CRTs) and Anzaldúan Chicana feminist theories to inform both our scholarly and political sensibilities. This trenza involves "the braiding of theory, qualitative research strategies, and sociopolitical consciousness for interacting with and gathering knowledge from" Chican@sLatin@s (Godinez, 2006, p. 26). It stresses the conviction of promoting social justice and is informed by our racialized and gendered ways of knowing, learning, and teaching. Critical race feminista praxis is born from our pedagogies of the home (Delgado Bernal, 2001), a Latin@ critical race theory sense of leadership and activism (Alemán, 2009a), and is weaved from different disciplines and multiple theoretical traditions (Acuña, 1988; Anzaldúa, 1987; Delgado & Stefancic, 1998; Haney-López, 1998; Montoya, 1994; D. G. Solórzano, 1998). It is an approach to partnership work that necessitates critical inquiry, sustained and authentic engagement with community, an intentionality of asset-based strategies, and the utilization of activist praxis.

Second, the trenza metaphor allows us to access and learn from the seminal works of cultural and queer theorist Gloria Anzaldúa (1987, 2000, 2005) and many other feminista scholars, who detail that our lives, experiences, and identities do not have to be and cannot be bifurcated from one another. In fact, they argue that it is essential to weave together our intellectual, political, and spiritual work (Ayala, 2008; Ayala, Herrera, Jiménez, & Lara, 2006; Burciaga & Tavares, 2006; Facio & Lara, 2014; Moraga, 2000; Prieto & Villenas, 2012). Rather than detaching and arbitrarily compartmentalizing our identities, we think of our personal, professional, and spiritual identities in academia, and more specifically in our methodological approach, as a trenza. Fusing strands of hair, weaving them in such a way that the strands come together to create something new, something that cannot exist without each of its parts, is how we understand our theoretical and methodological trenza (Delgado Bernal, 2008). The trenza is something that is whole and complete. Though as later chapters will detail, it is often a trenza greñuda (messy braid). It can only exist if separate parts are woven together; it symbolizes oneness and unity. Despite the fact that a local educational leader once said she was both confused and frustrated by the fluidity of our roles as parents, activists, and educational researchers, we understand that our work with Adelante has been naturally woven together by each of these and other identities.

What follows is a discussion of each theoretical strand and the trenza that emerges from braiding them together. We start the description of CRTs by highlighting the principles that fundamentally inform the partnership work we do. Next, we present Anzaldúan Chicana feminist ideas, including spiritual activism, nos/otras, choque, and nepantla, and how these ideas bring meaning to our 10-year partnership journey. Finally, we propose a critical race feminista praxis as the braiding of these two frameworks and introduce transformative ruptures as a crucial goal of this praxis. We also utilize Luis Urrieta's (2009) theorization of transas to talk about the strategies and tactics often needed within this type of praxis, and, more specifically, for the development of Adelante.

CRITICAL RACE THEORIES

Adelante's initial development and subsequent evolution is situated within the daily structural racisms that impact the educational experiences of Chican@Latin@ students in general, and at Jackson Elementary and its surrounding community in particular (see Chapter 1). In order to account for the systemic ways that coloniality (Americanization programs, English-only policies, tracking, denial of home languages and community histories, and so forth) shapes the (mis)education of Chican@sLatin@s, we rely on CRTs to address social (in)justice and the intersection of oppressions in U.S. society. Since the late 1990s (Ladson-Billings & Tate, 1997; D. G. Solórzano, 1998), scholars of color in the field of education have increasingly employed CRTs, including Latin@ critical race theory (LatCrit), critical race feminism (FemCrit), and tribal critical race theory (TribalCrit), in their research and practice (Lynn & Dixson, 2013). Considered comprehensively, the various CRTs in education might be understood as theoretical, conceptual, methodological, and pedagogical strategies that account for the role of race and racism in the U.S. educational system and frameworks that work toward the elimination of racism as part of a larger goal of eliminating all forms of subordination (D. G. Solórzano, 1998). Building from this understanding, LatCrit offers specific attention to issues such as bilingualism, immigration, citizenship, ethnicity, culture, identity, phenotype, sexuality, and history (Alemán, 2009a; Espinoza & Harris, 1998; Hernández-Truyol, 1998; Pérez Huber, 2009; Pérez Huber, Benavides Lopez, Malagon, Velez, & Solórzano, 2008; Solórzano & Delgado Bernal, 2001; Solórzano & Yosso, 2001a; Valdés, 1997). Both CRT and LatCrit challenge dominant discourses, privilege contextual and historical analyses, center the experiential knowledge of communities of color, commit to social justice, and recognize and argue for the centrality and intersectionality of racism in analysis (Solórzano & Yosso, 2001a). We briefly discuss some of these principles in relationship to our partnership work below.

One of CRT's basic theoretical principles requires scholars to challenge dominant ideologies and discourses. This means that CRTs confront the colonial logic that precludes the inclusion of non-Western, non-Eurocentric, and non-patriarchal knowledges into the curriculum (Calderón, 2014), as well as the deficit thinking that situates families and persons of color as lacking knowledge, history, and a desire to achieve. From a deficit stance, it is these families and persons who are responsible for student underachievement—because they "don't care," "don't value education," and because they "send their children to school unprepared" (Betsinger, García, & Guerra, 2001; García & Guerra, 2004; Olivos, 2007). Valencia and Solórzano (1997) refer to deficit thinking as a theory that places all the responsibility and accountability on students of color and blames their academic failure on supposed "internal deficits or deficiencies . . . [such as] limited intellectual abilities, linguistic shortcomings, lack of motivation to learn and immoral behavior" (p. 2). From this perspective, traditional explanations of school failure are decontextualized of the colonial histories, politics, economics, and cultural structures that play roles in creating inaccessible and inequitable pathways. Deficit thinking not only persists in the professional lives of teachers, but also permeates school buildings such as Jackson Elementary. CRTs as analytical frameworks, thus, help us challenge the colonial logic of deficit thinking that is present within partnership work and disrupt the inequitable educational pathways in this local community.

Privileging contextual and historical descriptions over abstract or ahistorical ones is another important principle of CRTs. Therefore, both our scholarship and approach to developing the partnership rely heavily on analyzing educational policies and practices, and on contextualizing educational outcomes by placing them in both a historical and contemporary context (Bell, 2004; Delgado & Stefancic, 2001). For example, to understand the (mis)education of Chican@s one must understand the history of the 2,000-mile United States–Mexico border, as its creation marks the beginning of the differentiation of people of Mexican descent (Elenes, 2011). This colonial history is based in ideologies of racial superiority (Acuña, 1988) and racist nativism (Pérez Huber, 2009) and is informed by European and American imperialism (Montejano, 1987). In the previous chapter, we provided a historical and contemporary context specifically related to Utah's economic and educational gaps for Chican@sLatin@s. These are the contemporary remnants of that colonial border history: by-products that can be linked to ongoing colonial practices such as de facto school segregation (Orfield, Kucsera, & Siegel-Hawley, 2012), unequal educational funding (Alemán, 2007; Darling-Hammond, 2007; Ladson-Billings, 2006), and the misguided expectation that culturally diverse student populations will be successful in educational environments that are culturally unresponsive (Ladson-Billings, 2009).

Because colonial logic has imposed a Eurocentric authority over ways of knowing in Indigenous communities and communities of color (Smith, 1999), the recentering of knowledges produced within communities of color is yet another important principle of CRTs. Many educational practices are the result of a coloniality that shapes the organization, governance, curricula, and assessment of schooling in ways that allow Western narratives to become accepted as universal truths, marginalizing the knowledge of "others" (Smith, 1999; Tuck & Yang, 2012). Indeed, schools have played a vital role in the systematic, often brutal, denial of heritage languages, histories, knowledges, and cultures (Calderón, 2014). Our experiential knowledge, and that of Jackson families, has deeply informed and shaped the partnership, and guided our development of Adelante programming such as the Oral History Project, ballet folklórico classes, and the after-school ethnic studies class (all described in the next chapter). In this way, the communal and familial knowledges, language, histories, stories, and culture, shared from the knowers and creators, are incorporated as valid and vital to the education of Jackson students (Delgado Bernal, 2002). The knowledges of communities of color and our approach to countering the majoritarian narratives that abound across societal institutions have also shaped our specific methods of data collection (Alemán, Delgado Bernal, & Mendoza, 2013; Duncan, 2002; Guajardo & Guajardo, 2004; Ladson-Billings & Donner, 2005; Solórzano & Yosso, 2001a; Stovall, 2005), as we have relied on more than 160 interviews and pláticas to better understand the experiences of the students, mentors, and parents within the Adelante community.

Finally, perhaps one of the most important theoretical principles of CRTs is the centrality of racism and its intersection with other forms of subordination. Critical race and legal scholar Derrick Bell names the acknowledgment and acceptance of the centrality and pervasiveness of racism in society as racial realism, the notion that racism is a permanent aspect of our society, embedded in the everyday lives of all persons in the United States, and corrosive to all of society's institutions and structures (Bell, 1995). We adhere to this notion that racism is not just haphazard or individual, but rather is embedded structurally into society's institutions and systems, and within policies such as those that impact health care, housing, criminal justice, immigration, legal citizenship, and in this case, education (Bell, 1992; Crenshaw, Gotanda, Peller, & Thomas, 1995). For schools in particular, macro-level institutionalized racism creates inequities that not only manifest as systemic "gaps" in educational achievement, but also result in micro-level individual gaps in the K–16 educational pipeline that are part of the Chican@Latin@ diasporic educational experience (Alemán, 2007; Ladson-Billings, 1998; D. G. Solórzano, 1998).

Institutionalized racism is not only characterized by race; it is also based on ethnicity, language, color, gender, sexuality, poverty, and immigration status (Oliva, Pérez, & Parker, 2013; Teranishi & Pazich, 2013; Tijerina Revilla, 2004). For example, educational theorist Lindsay Pérez Huber (2009) points to how racist nativism negatively impacts the schooling of Latin@ students and frames undocumented Latin@ immigrants as problematic, burdensome, and "illegal." She also addresses how this form of racism is gendered, as it frames undocumented Latinas as burdensome women who come to the United States to have "anchor babies" that will be supported by U.S. social services (Pérez Huber, 2015). Many of the parents we have worked with over the past decade are immigrant mothers who regularly experience this type of gendered racism.

Collectively, these principles of CRTs have undergirded the infrastructure of Adelante and shaped its development, growth, and sustainability. For example, explicitly grounding Adelante as a partnership that promotes a "college-going culture" is one way to implement CRTs' challenge to dominant ideologies. It was our intention to establish Adelante as a counter to the majoritarian narrative and deficit-based ideologies that exist around the educability of Brown students. In addition, the partnership's activities and programs are designed with a goal of collective community transformation that is directly related to the social justice principle that CRTs promote. CRTs have guided our program development, informed our tactics for sustaining the numerous partnership initiatives, and ultimately, solidified our rationale for doing the work. In the next section, we introduce the Chicana feminist ideas that we braid together with the principles of CRTs.

CHICANA FEMINIST THEORIES

[A Chicana feminist] theoretical framework embodies the goals of advocacy scholarship, which both challenges the claims of objectivity and links research to community concerns and social change. . . . I suggest that creating bridges between the production of knowledge in the academic world and communities struggling for social justice is absolutely fundamental. Thus, I cannot remove myself from the research process and must instead place myself in the center among those involved in creating this knowledge.

—Téllez, 2005, p. 49

To understand our methodology—meaning the theory and sensibilities that have guided the evolution of our research and program development with Adelante—we turn to Anzaldúan Chicana feminist theories. We understand that adopting a Chicana feminist perspective in educational research embodies the goals of advocacy scholarship and is more than just adopting a theoretical lens, becoming familiar with a literature, learning corresponding methods, and analyzing data. It also embodies who we are and requires us to grapple with our activist scholar roles, embrace alternative ways of knowing, and confront those aspects of ourselves that render us the colonized or the perpetrator, particularly when we are working with marginalized communities, including immigrant, queer, youth, and people of color (Calderón, Delgado Bernal, Velez, Pérez Huber, & Malagon, 2012). For example, although we are insiders who have lived in this neighborhood and have children who attended this school, we are also positioned as outsiders, with numerous privileges afforded by location of birth and generational rights denied to many families in the community we have been a part of. We hold contradictory identities as colonizer and colonized and, as Villenas (1996) states, we are both and neither: We "have a foot in both worlds; in the dominant privileged institutions and in the marginalized communities" (p. 231).

Chicana feminist scholarship disrupts Western colonial assumptions such as the ideas that research needs to be neutral or unbiased and that our bodymindspirit (Lara, 2002) must be separate entities. Initially, neither of us explicitly named our methodology as Chicana feminist as we talked with community members, classroom teachers, or university gatekeepers about initiating Adelante. Yet, this epistemological orientation has informed and shaped every aspect of my (Dolores's) engagement with Adelante, and it has more recently given me (Enrique) needed analytical tools and the language to talk about my activist scholar identities.

For example, in reflecting on how we have approached our anticolonial research for over a decade, Anzaldúa's (2002) notion of spiritual activism helps us describe the way we have brought our bodymindspirit to our praxis. Anzaldúa offers a holistic worldview that merges social activism with spiritual vision, "a way of life and a call to action. . . . Spiritual activism is spirituality for social change" (Keating, 2006, p. 11). Spiritual activism "connects one with the world . . . a way of understanding one's place in the world and working toward transformation of inequities" (Elenes, 2011, p. 136). In this way, our anticolonial work with Adelante has been an intellectual, political, and spiritual pursuit of educational transformation, while simultaneously nurturing our respective souls.

This suturing of the mind, body, and soul provides us with a way to forefront and affirm the Brown body while simultaneously understanding how it is "othered," regulated, and governed in schools and society. Cruz (2006) points out that "the incorporation of the brown body in the discussions about representation, social control, and the constructions of normality" (p. 68) is crucial to educational research. Jackson Elementary is overflowing with Brown bodies—parents, children, college student mentors, the graduate students we worked with, and our own. There were times when our collective Brown bodies were "othered" by the predominantly White teaching staff, and though it was never explicitly stated to us in this way, it was clear that with some teachers, there was a level of discomfort with all the educated Brown bodies in the school. Perhaps that is because the collective presence of the undergraduate mentors and Adelante graduate students counters society's colonial deficit thinking and the dominant myth that says youth of color do not care about school or are incapable of succeeding academically (Valencia & Black, 2002). As we will discuss in Chapter 4, the surveillance of Brown bodies came to a head with a discipline policy that regulated the bodies of elementary school students and unleashed the agency of Brown immigrant, Spanish-speaking mothers.

Indeed, Anzaldúa (2000) offers the concept of nos/otras as a way to theorize the need to bridge commonalities among the differently situated bodies within Adelante (including Mexican immigrant parents, their children, White middle-class teachers, and Chican@ middle-class professors). *Nosotras* is the Spanish word for the feminine *we*, and it indicates a collectivity or type of group identity. Anzaldúa splits the word into two, which both affirms this collectivity, but also acknowledges the divisiveness that is so often felt between groups of people; *nos* implies "us," and *otras* implies "otherness." For Anzaldúa, joining the *nos* plus *otras* together leads to the possibility of healing. "We contain the others, the others contain us" (Keating, 2006, p. 10).

The relationships within Jackson have sometimes been tenuous, and we give examples in Chapter 4 of strategies and practices that bridged the vastly different cultural realities, even if momentarily, between teachers and their students and their students' families. In these instances, nos/otras gives us a way to transcend the "us versus them" mentality (Anzaldúa, 2000).

Anzaldúa's conceptualizations of choque and nepantla are additional inter-connected concepts that are helpful in guiding and making sense of our praxis. She describes choques as the collisions that occur when "two self-consistent but habitually incompatible frames of reference" collide (Anzaldúa, 1987, p. 78). For example, in Chapter 4 we discuss the choque that occurs when the deficit thinking that is prevalent in the school community collides with the asset-based thinking that Adelante attempts to institutionalize. Choques are the initial collisions that can often shift one into a tension-filled space of nepantla (Anzaldúa, 2005).

Nepantla is a Nahuatl word referring to the space between two worlds or the land in the middle. It is the liminal middle ground between worlds, identities, and realities, which means it is also a space of contradiction, dissonance, transition, and—perhaps most important—possibility. In fact, Keating (2006) reminds us that "[n]epantla is painful, messy, confusing, and chaotic. . . ." And at times, "nepantla hurts!!!!" (p. 9). But from this space of confusion and dissonance can come growth, transformation, or new knowledge. Anzaldúa uses the term *nepantla* to refer to identity-related issues as well as intellectual and epistemological contradictions, conflicts, tensions, and growth. In Chapter 5, nepantla allows us to theorize about the multiple, complex, and shifting identities of the college student of color who mentored the Jackson students.

Methodologically, nepantla has also been particularly useful for us to explore and embrace the tensions, contradictions, and mistakes of our praxis. Anzaldúa (2002) argues that it is in nepantla where we often spend most of our time and that it might be advantageous to call nepantla "home." Our methodological perspective embraces nepantla as home, where practice and theory meet and often grate against each other (Alemán, Delgado Bernal, & Mendoza, 2013). This requires researchers to be nepantler@s, the bridge builders or "threshold people" (Keating, 2006, p. 9) who have a tolerance for ambiguity. Elenes (2011) says nepantler@s are constantly shifting "from single goal reasoning to divergent thinking. This shift is characterized by a movement away from set patterns and goals and toward a holistic perspective . . ." (p. 51). In many ways, we, and the graduate students who have worked with us, are nepantler@s who have constantly negotiated and shifted between meeting the overarching goals of Adelante, working within the institutional constraints of educational institutions, and collaborating with students, parents, and families who struggle with everyday realities. We return to a discussion of this methodological home of nepantla in the final chapter.

CRITICAL RACE FEMINISTA PRAXIS

Our critical race feminista praxis is the coming together, the braiding and the weaving, of critical race and Chicana feminist theories and the strategies and approaches we applied in our practice. In developing and coordinating the partnership for over a decade and in making sense of our research, we, like other scholars, have been informed by and worked toward a merging and an alignment of these two theories (Alemán, Delgado Bernal, & Mendoza, 2013; Pérez Huber, 2009; Tijerina Revilla, 2004). Conveying a simple, straightforward, or linear process and outcome is not our goal. It has been anything but that. Rather, throughout the book we articulate how we reached toward, struggled with, and evolved into a critical race feminista praxis. Here, we offer a working conceptualization of this praxis as one that is undeniably guided by an awareness of permanent, indestructible racism (Bell, 1992), but also one that is guided by and embraced as a constant state of in-between-ness, conflict, frustration, and liminality (Anzaldúa, 1987, 2002). Shaped by an awareness of the ways in which young Brown female, male, and gender queer bodies have been "othered" and regulated, our praxis reminds us to affirm the wisdom and experiences of those Brown bodies. It is a praxis motivated by a yearning to rupture heterosexist, racist, anti-immigrant, classist, and patriarchal structures while simultaneously pushing us toward a spiritual activism.

Guided by critical race feminista praxis, we are now able to articulate our understanding of what we call "transformative ruptures." We propose transformative ruptures as those incidents, interactions, experiences, and moments where a disruption of pervasive coloniality, institutional racism, and systemic inequity occurs. They are the spaces in which roses can grow from cracks in the concrete (Duncan-Andrade, 2009; Shakur, 1999) and the realization that opportunities for change and possibility can emerge when choques between mindsets, discourses, ideologies, and politics arise (Anzaldúa, 2002). Although the larger structural and institutional inequities such as racism remain solidified, there is a hope, and in fact, an understanding that transformative ruptures can multiply, breeding coalitional resistance and a progression toward more equitable and just policies, practices, and outcomes.

An example of a transformative rupture is related to our earlier mention of some teachers' discomfort with Brown educated bodies in the school. We came to understand the presence of college students of color, both undergraduates and graduate, as a disruption to a space where deficit discourses were prevalent and high academic expectations were not the norm. In one instance, walking down the hallway toward a classroom with five Chicana graduate research assistants, all future PhDs, the unease and body language of one teacher and a staff member seemed to be provoked by our collective presence. In reality, our collective, physical presence did nothing to alter the material realities of the students or families at Jackson, nor did it dismantle the structural inequality that exists in U.S. schools or the inequity that remains at Jackson. However, as we demonstrate in upcoming chapters, the presence of the undergraduate and graduate students of color was a transformative rupture to the culture of the school.

How does one engage in a critical race feminista praxis? To partially answer that question and make sense of how we developed and sustained Adelante for so long, we utilize Urrieta's (2009) understanding of transas as the day-to-day practices of Chican@ activist educators who struggle to make "whitestream" educational institutions more equitable and just spaces. Transas include the calculated practices, moves, and plays that are sometimes strategic, situational, or improvisational. They involve strategizing and making calculated decisions in terms of what issues are worth battling for, but they are also influenced by innovation and spontaneity. Urrieta (2009) states that the daily practices of Chican@ activist educators require one to "straddle roles as institutional agents and activists, both colonizer and colonized, opening doors and also functioning as gatekeepers" (p. 163). Therefore, to engage in transas requires an awareness of the ambiguity of one's activist educator identity and of shifting power dynamics. Urrieta draws on Anzaldúa to point to a third space of possibility where Chican@ activist educators inhabit a hybrid, contradictory space that means seeing through "neither the serpent's nor the eagle's eyes, but both—a unique hybrid space from which to work change into the system from within" (p. 164). We understand this contradictory space as Anzaldúa's nepantla and Chican@ activist scholars as nepantler@s who engage in transas daily from within educational institutions in pursuit of transformative ruptures to inequitable structures.

We also understand transas to be the strategizing and the myriad responses to the racialized, gendered, and colonial landscapes that activist educators confront. Arguing that they are responses that first and foremost center the interests of students and communities of color, our understanding and application of Urrieta's transas calls for maneuvering against the many forms of inequity and discrimination that constantly operate in educational institutions. This idea of transas helps us name the countless approaches we used to maneuver within both higher education and K–12 educational systems in developing and institutionalizing Adelante. Our transas have been organized, planned, spontaneous, and not always successful. Our transas also evolved as our sensibilities became more attuned with university bureaucracies, student and family needs, the experiences of the students, the culture of the school, and the expectations of the teachers.

One transa that we often employed was strategically using the language and goals of the university or K–12 education when garnering support for different components of Adelante. For example, in Chapter 5, we describe some of our transas at the university level, including how we developed relationships with university stakeholders and allied the mentoring component of Adelante with the university's Community Engagement classification by the Carnegie Foundation. These were part of the calculated daily practices that drew upon our nepantler@ roles as activist scholars who are keenly aware of the permanence and ubiquity of racism.

There is a clear connection between our transas and the transformative ruptures that occurred. Our transas were employed with the expectation that they would yield transformative ruptures. This was certainly true for the Chican@ activist educators in Urrieta's (2009) study, whose "day-to-day practices were embedded with the hope that their practices would lead to what some referred to as a 'domino effect' or a 'ripple effect' to bring about larger societal change" (p. 113). Transformative ruptures are a way to theorize the ripple effects in that they are grounded in CRT's understanding of pervasive structural inequities and Anzaldúa's possibility for transformation within the fissures of conflict and choques.

In the next section, we move from transas, transformative ruptures, and the theory of critical race feminista praxis to the actual practice of Adelante by very briefly introducing the different program elements.

ADELANTE'S PROGRAM ELEMENTS

Deeply informed by critical race feminista praxis, Adelante is premised on the idea that all students should have the expectation of college attendance from their earliest public school stage, kindergarten. We remind the reader that Adelante's main objectives from the beginning have been (1) to prepare students and their families for college by integrating higher education into their school experience, and (2) to help establish a college-going culture within the school. Within the partnership, five interrelated components are central to meeting the objectives of Adelante. These five components include university mentoring, university visits, cultural and academic enrichment, parental and teacher engagement, and research for change (see Figure 2.1). We do not discuss these here, because we describe them in detail in upcoming chapters. Instead, we provide the reader with a visual representation of the major components we will address.

Figure 2.1. Adelante Components

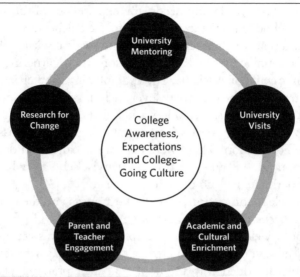

We do, however, note that these components emerged and developed over time, sometimes based on teacher feedback, parent requests, university resources, or graduate students' academic and experiential knowledge. We cannot overstate the importance of the relational aspect in how these components improved and matured over time. The reciprocal (and yet sometimes fractured) relationships that the Adelante graduate assistants and we formed with school staff and leaders, university officials, college mentors, and especially with elementary school students and their parents were crucial to the development of each of these interrelated components.

Many educational books promise a fix-all solution or model that will reform education. We do not offer Adelante as this type of promise. Chican@Latin@ students, families, and communities too often become the recipients of the newest model of reform, sometimes with tragic ramifications. We do not believe the Adelante partnership or any other partnership, project, or model, for that matter, can eradicate educational inequities. And yet, we, like many other critical educators, engage in spiritual activism on a never-ending journey toward eradicating educational equities. Motivated by spiritual activism and using transas, we maneuver through the barriers, mistakes, tensions, and compromises that are necessary in an inequitable and stratified educational environment—the nepantla space from which transformative ruptures and learning can occur. In the next chapter, we address the transformative ruptures of L@s Primer@s in the face of racial realism and everyday educational inequities.

CHAPTER THREE

L@S PRIMER@S

I have a T-shirt that says "future college student." So, yeah, I am going to college.

—Ana, kindergarten student, 2005

There have been 10 cohorts of kindergartners who have participated in Adelante. L@s Primer@s, the first cohort, consists of the 37 students we have tried to maintain relationships with throughout the years.[1] Today, L@s Primer@s are in high school, but on a crisp day in September 2005, they were 5- and 6-year-olds who eagerly loaded onto the bus for their first field trip to the University of Utah. At the time, they did not realize they would visit the university nearly 50 times before moving on to middle school or that they would meet and get to know so many first-generation college students who came from similar backgrounds. Instead, as they fidgeted on the 15-minute drive to the university, they were likely thinking about how long it would be before they could eat their sack lunch or if they could get the window seat on the ride back home.

When they and about 20 parent chaperones arrived on campus, they exited the bus to find a welcoming group of faculty and students that included one dean and a campus vice president. One of the kindergarten teachers was almost emotional as she said something like, "Look how special they think you are because they are all here to greet you." The kids jumped, walked, and skipped two by two, holding hands through the reception line as they received balloons and a goody bag with university paraphernalia. After a brief welcome, the group split up, with half going to the library and half going to the football stadium, and then switching locations later. While at the library one mother whispered, "Aquí es a donde vas a venir cuando tú vayas a la universidad." ("Here is where you will come when you go to the university.") Throughout the morning, the students were excited, talkative, and observant. They asked great questions like, "Which one of these buildings is the university?" and "Has anybody ever read every book in this library?" When it was time to load the bus back up, we could see L@s

Primer@s were worn out, and one of their teachers mentioned later that a few even fell asleep on the way back to school. Although we knew it had been a great kickoff for Adelante, we did not realize at the time that these trips and other Adelante programs, such as ballet folklórico[2] or the Oral History Project, would impact this group of students and ultimately the school culture. We also did not realize that the next decade would bring so many challenges that sometimes led to small but meaningful transformative ruptures and, at other times, led to so much remaining the same.

In this chapter, we share some of what L@s Primer@s remember about their participation in different components of Adelante, especially in relation to the college mentors, the Oral History Project, and field trips. These different components of Adelante have been a means to create a college-going culture and awareness of college, to center the familial knowledge of L@s Primer@s, and to build upon students' self-worth. By describing the different Adelante components that L@s Primer@s remembered after leaving Jackson, we provide examples of how we operationalized Adelante's founding principles and objectives, discussed in the previous chapter. Just as important, based on the reflections of L@s Primer@s and 10 years' worth of qualitative data, we argue that Adelante has had an impact on the school culture and on students who now consider college part of their future educational trajectories and understand themselves as creators and holders of knowledge (Delgado Bernal, 2002). Though the next section celebrates the highlights of our 10-year story, it is followed by some of the deep and ongoing challenges that limit educational expectations, access, and academic outcomes for students at Jackson.

WHAT DID THEY TAKE AWAY FROM ADELANTE?

In the spring of 2014, right before L@s Primer@s were transitioning to their freshman year of high school, we invited them to join us for one of three pláticas at the Jackson library to reflect on their Adelante experiences and their upcoming transition to high school. This would be the fourth time we interviewed them since they were kindergartners. We invited all 17 who attended Bryant Middle School, a Title I, racially/ethnically diverse school that Jackson feeds into, to share their memories and reflections. Thirteen participated. A few were eager and happy to speak with us; others were pressured by parents who knew us well, or by their former ballet folklórico teacher, Cinthia Cervantes-Castañeda, who was one of our graduate students. The group included four boys and nine girls, all of them Latin@, except for one mixed-race student. Of the Latin@ students, one is undocumented, nine are children of immigrants, one is fifth-generation Mexican American, and one is from a mixed generation family.

PORTRAITS: A LOOK AT TWO OF L@S PRIMER@S

Over the years, we interacted with L@s Primer@s and their parents in numerous ways, sometimes related specifically to Adelante and other times related to the fact that they were the friends of Enrique's daughter or Dolores's son. These interactions occurred in places such as soccer games, picnics, ballet folklórico performances, birthday parties, field trips, political demonstrations, the community garden, and within the school. Before we share what L@s Primer@s say collectively at the pláticas, we provide a small portrait of two of the students—one girl, Catalina, and one boy, Rubén. We chose these two students because we came to know them and their families particularly well and they represent two vastly different experiences within this group of students while providing insight into the amazing young people and families in the Jackson community.

Rubén was a small, skinny, güero (light-skinned) boy with a kind heart who arrived at Jackson during the second semester of his kindergarten year. His family had recently migrated from Jalisco, Mexico, via California, and they were undocumented. Shortly after he arrived, he told the story of how he and his mother crossed the border to two of his Adelante mentors, both who were immigrants and one who had also crossed the border with her mother over a decade earlier. He described how he and his family were incarcerated and expressed fear, humiliation, and resentment toward "los puercos policías." Rubén's mother has an 8th-grade education, and though his father, Francisco, worked in construction, he completed technical school in Mexico and earned a certificate in hotel administration and food service. Rubén has two older sisters and Rubén's parents have always been very supportive of his schooling. Francisco once shared with us his dream for Rubén and his two daughters: "Mis sueños para mis hijos son que no hagan lo que yo hice, siempre mas mejor que yo, mas arriba." ("My dreams for my kids are that they will not do what I did. Always be better than me, much higher.") Rubén usually kept away from extramural sports, but he danced in the Adelante ballet folklórico group from kindergarten through 6th grade. In 6th grade, he was a member of student government, and in middle school, he was in honors classes and the AVID[3] class. As an adolescent, Rubén came out, and by his freshman year he had a boyfriend that he recognized publicly. When he was very young, he always said he wanted to be a doctor so he could help poor people. Later, he talked about being a chef, and upon entering high school his aspirations changed to wanting to be a fashion designer. During the plática, he started off a little quieter than normal. Throughout the interview, he was very reflective, sharing his dreams, concerns for the future, and how he and his classmates had changed over time.

Catalina was a cute 5-year-old girl with a round face and thick hair who sometimes wore braids. She is an only child and was born in South America. Her grandma still lives there and sometimes comes to visit. When Catalina was in kindergarten, her mother, Lourdes, shared with us how pleased she was that Catalina was participating in Adelante: "Ella ahorita está conociendo la universidad. Se esta familiarizando con lo que sería en el futuro." ("Right now she's getting to know the university. She's familiarizing herself with what she'll be in the future.") Lourdes, a single mother and a professional with formal training in technology from her home country, was active in the school and very supportive of Catalina's education. In speaking about her own educational experiences, she longed for her daughter to have college opportunities. In elementary school, Catalina often shared her excitement about the field trips, mentors, and summer camps with her mom, and she danced in the ballet folklórico group. In middle school, she was in honors classes and AVID, and she expressed her feelings of pride not only for her bilingualism but also for her biliteracy. During her freshman year, Catalina had an elaborate quinceañera with a red theme and a formal dinner at a local salón. Enrique's family attended, as did one of Adelante's former graduate assistants and four of L@s Primer@s, including Rubén, who was a chambelán. During the plática, Catalina had much to say and often led the conversation. She shared that she did not have experiences in middle school with teachers discouraging her or holding low expectations, but many of her friends did because of the stereotypes about Latin@s. She said she planned to go to college so she can be someone who is "breaking those stereotypes."

As Catalina, Rubén, and the other students entered the room for one of our pláticas, some of them made comments about how small the chairs were, how familiar the space was, or how they had not been in the school since they finished 6th grade 2 years earlier. With pizza and drinks, we started off by sharing video clips of them in kindergarten and in 4th grade. There was some laughter, embarrassment, silence, and gentle teasing as they watched their younger selves, often wearing red T-shirts that said "Adelante" on front and "Future College Student" on back. Some of them had not talked to one another in quite a while, as a result of making new friends in middle school. Because of this, each plática started off a little awkward and quiet, but as the students watched the videos and began to make comments, it was clear that they were all tied together through their participation in Adelante and in the Spanish dual-immersion program at Jackson.

MENTORS: EMBODYING THE MESSAGE
OF BROWN COLLEGE STUDENTS

As we talked, students began to recall memories about elementary school generally and Adelante more specifically. They fondly remembered former mentors, especially those college students who mentored for consecutive years.[4] They were aware that most of the mentors were the first in their families to go to college and that the mentors were students of color who often came from similar schools and neighborhoods as they did. Overwhelmingly, L@s Primer@s agreed that having college student mentors had an impact on how they were introduced to college and how they thought about the possibility of college for themselves. Genoveva pointed to the interactions with college students: "When we were in elementary, we were friends with the mentors. When they came, we'd get really excited to see them. We would have conversations with them." These conversations were often about school and going to college. Kati remembered how she and others learned about college because the mentors sometimes talked about their classes and the homework or projects they were working on. And sometimes the conversations were just about life and what the mentors were doing outside of school. Though Catalina remembered one mentor telling her about a Wiz Khalifah concert, L@s Primer@s mostly remembered how the college students inspired them to be "more motivated to go to college." As Jacquelin stated, the college mentors' presence showed us "what we can do and how." The mentors were so important to Quetzal that when asked what part of Adelante he would want to take with him to high school, he said the mentors because they "show me the way and just explain stuff to me."

There is something very deliberate, very conspicuous, and very tangible about having college students of color, their Brown bodies, walk the halls and be present in classrooms on a daily basis throughout the school year. We understand the presence of Brown bodies as mentors and role models to be a transformative rupture that sends a powerful message of ethnic/racial and academic affirmation to the Jackson students. Because "[n]othing provokes the custodians of normality and objectification more than the excessiveness of a body" (Cruz, 2006, p. 62), the weekly presence of college students of color is clearly a disruption to dominant societal beliefs that do not consider Chican@Latin@ students as knowledge producers, intellectuals, or future college students.

Oral History Project: (Re)Centering the Marginalized Knowledge of Communities of Color

We also asked L@s Primer@s what they remembered about the activities they completed each year in the Oral History Project. These are literacy-based activities that draw from familial knowledge and have been developed by Adelante graduate research assistants in collaboration with classroom teachers. The goal has always been to maintain high academic standards while aligning learning outcomes with the core curriculum via culturally relevant projects that allow students to value who they are and where they come from.[5] L@s Primer@s held positive memories, but interestingly, as they reflected on some of the many projects, they did not remember it as a time of real schoolwork, but rather, they thought "it was a nice break from school." They said it was something "fun" and "not boring." In talking about the time that was designated to do the oral history activities, Monica said:

> I thought it was different. It was more fun than what we're usually doing, and we were more involved with it. It wasn't like we just had to sit down and learn. . . . We got to choose what we wanted and all this stuff.

For example, Monica might be remembering that in 3rd grade, L@s Primer@s completed two oral history projects, both of which involved interviewing and talking to parents or elders in their family. One of those, a genealogy project, required the students to create a family tree, gather family photos, and after interviewing family members of their choice, write a family history in Spanish or English. They wrote drafts, received feedback, and edited their work until the final stories were ready to be part of a class book. L@s Primer@s learned much about their families, and the narratives they wrote were funny, sad, or happy as they described their parent's migration to the United States across the desert, a great-grandpa in World War II, great-grandparents who had passed away, a grandma who was sick, or the hard workers in their family.

When Bradley reflected back on what he had learned he said, "I found out new things about where I was from. The things I did not know about myself." Catalina remembered interviewing her tía and using one of her grandmother's stories. Many of the narratives the students wrote demonstrated their pride and love for their family with comments such as "Me siento muy orgullosa de ser miembro de esta familia." ("I feel very proud to be a member of this family.") Another stated, "Yo también estoy orgullosa de mis padres, los quiero mucho y nunca olvidaré lo que hacen por mí." ("I also am proud of my parents, I love them very much and I'll never forget what they have done for me.") Each year after the students completed a project and had practiced presenting their work with their peers and teacher, they shared their work at a "public" book reading, video showcase, or gallery stroll in the library. These were multigenerational events with food and drinks and were always well attended. As they recalled these public showcases, Bradley fondly remembered reading his story to the audience: "I remember talking in the microphone . . . telling them about myself."

Obviously, the histories and lives of students of color, immigrant students, and marginalized communities within the United States are not well represented in school curriculum (Delpit, 1995; Kohli & Solórzano, 2012; Ladson-Billings, 2001; Sleeter, 2001). An education that is disconnected from one's lived experiences and history further excludes and marginalizes the lives and knowledge of Chican@Latin@ students in particular. These exclusions also reify the perception of Chican@Latin@ students as empty vessels who do not possess cultural, familial, raced, or gendered knowledge and, therefore, cannot be viewed as contributing members in the classrooms. Making familial knowledge the foundation of the Oral History Project not only responds to CRT's call to (re)center the marginalized knowledge of Adelante families, but also allows students to actually enjoy learning that is rigorous, critical, and "not boring." In many ways, the Oral History Project contributes to the ethnic/racial affirmation that is at the core of the partnership, and this translates into students who see themselves as holders of knowledge and as future college students.

In previous scholarship (Flores Carmona & Delgado Bernal, 2012), we also argue that the Oral History Project became a tool that at times strengthened the communication and solidarity between families and some of the teachers. It served as a way to bridge the children's cultural realities with those of their teachers by transcending an "us" and "them" mentality and bringing nos/otras together (Anzaldúa, 2000). That is, it allowed teachers to hear and learn about the struggles and the dreams of their students and their parents. Although not all teachers have participated in the Oral History Project and not all of them have been impacted in the same way, there are teachers like Mrs. Hope, who said:

> The particular project helped me to better understand the relationship that
> my students and their parents have. Many of the interview answers were very

touching and helped me to see how much they love and value their children. It helped me to want to be a better teacher for their child. (Flores Carmona & Delgado Bernal, 2012, p. 114)

In this way, the Oral History Project not only disrupts normalized core curriculum by enacting CRT's principle of recentering marginalized knowledges, but it can also strengthen the family–teacher relationship. This, Anzaldúa says, moves us from nos/otras toward a collectivity of no-sotras, where "[w]e contain the others, the others contain us" (Keating, 2006, p. 10).

Field Trips: Envisioning Oneself as a Future College Student

Since 2005, Adelante has provided regular and consistent field trips to an educational institution that was not created to serve Chican@Latin@ students (Pizarro, 2005; Valenzuela, 1999; Yosso, 2006). These trips were neither accidental nor inconsequential. By visiting so regularly, we hoped that Jackson students would become comfortable in university spaces and that the campus would become so familiar that they could imagine their future selves in college.[6]

During our pláticas, L@s Primer@s reflected on a few of the nearly 50 visits to the university that they took during elementary school, and several of them said the trips were what they remembered most from their Adelante experiences. Some of them reminisced about that first field trip to the library and football field; others remembered participating in Kids' Court[7] at the law school, dissecting a cow's heart at the medical school, dancing with faculty and students in a modern dance class, or visiting the dorms where college students lived. Susana explained that she liked these trips to the university because they showed her what she and her classmates would be able to do when they are in college: "It was pretty fun, the field trips and all that. I like how we would go to the university. It really shows . . . what we can do in those classes, like what we can be able to do in college."

Over the years, we have heard many students echo Susana and talk about "when I go to college. . . ." One field trip to the University of Utah dormitories in particular stands out to us because Joslin, a 3rd-grader at the time, made a simple statement to Judi Pérez-Torres, an Adelante graduate assistant, that made us all realize how L@s Primer@s, even back in the 3rd grade, were beginning to envision themselves as future college students. The following vignette of this visit to the dorms with L@s Primer@s reveals the ways students began visualizing themselves as college students as a result of the Adelante field trips.

Touring the undergraduate dorms on a crisp fall morning, Joslin was excited to see where college students lived, where they ate breakfast and lunch, and how close they were to the classrooms where they learned. Having already visited the university more than 20 times in her first four years of elementary school, Joslin liked learning to make slime from Chemistry professor, Dr. Neil Smith, but was grossed out when she and her classmates were given the opportunity to touch a cow's brain during the activity that was led by 3rd-year medical students in the U's College of Medicine. This trip was different though. It opened up a whole new area of the university that she had not yet visited and prompted her to envision herself living on campus.

The elementary students were excited as they checked out all the fun stuff that students had access to when living on campus and many questions were prompted. Can students choose one of their friends to room with? Did students have access to the game room all the time? Could students select any of the various food options, including desserts, while visiting the huge cafeteria? Did everyone have their own TV and mini fridge in his or her dorm? And after seeing the way rooms were decorated differently, including one where soccer and football posters and the flag of Mexico adorned the walls, could students decorate as they wished? Joslin mentioned to Judi, "I'm going to be roommates with Berta when we come to the U and I'm going to have a purple bedspread and lots of pillows." (Alemán, Pérez-Torres, & Oliva, 2013, p. 19)

Anzaldúa (1987) says, "Nothing happens in the 'real' world unless it first happens in the images in our heads" (p. 87). So although we do not yet know how many of the hundreds of students who have participated in Adelante will go to college, what we do know is that Joslin and many other students have begun to imagine a "real" world in which they are future college students. Hearing Joslin, as a 3rd-grader, talk about who she will room with and how she will decorate her dorm room might seem trivial to some and not a significant "outcome" for educational research. However, we understand the significance of young people from communities with unequal educational opportunities dreaming about their future realities. These types of transformative ruptures are crucial in the face of historical legacies of educational inequity that young people face, and they align with the way CRTs challenge dominant ideologies and discourses about who belongs—and who does not belong—on college campuses.

Exposure to Higher Education: Aspiring to Go to College

Toward the end of each plática, we asked L@s Primer@s if they felt their elementary school experiences were different from those of most of their friends in middle school who did not go to Jackson. They all said yes. They were well aware that their exposure to the different Adelante activities was something that most of their peers in middle school had not had access to in elementary school. Bradley said, "Most elementary schools don't have the opportunity to take kids at a young age . . . to a university." Catalina elaborated on this point when she recounted a recent field trip to the university and what happened when one of her middle school teachers asked, "Oh, how many of you have ever been to a college campus? How many have been to the U?" She said that the few former Adelante students raised their hands, but most of the other students did not. Very casually Catalina told us, "I've been there. It was nothing new to me." Quetzal summed up the exposure L@s Primer@s had to higher education when he said, "I would not have known half of the stuff about college if I wouldn't have been in Adelante."

All the students felt they knew more about college than their middle school friends did, and all of them stated that they wanted to go to college. Their aspirations covered a range of careers, including a pediatrician, scientist, fashion designer, architect, anesthesiologist, and a chef who owns her own restaurant. Even for those students who were not sure what they wanted to do, there seemed to be a clear sense that college meant you would get to pursue something you liked to do as opposed to something you had to do in order to make a living like many of their parents had to do. Rogelio said, "To get an education, to do something that you like to do, and . . . do it for a long time, that's what I want to do." Similarly, in one of the pláticas, Kati became emotional when she reflected on how she had been guided to think about pursuing something she is passionate about: "You guys (Adelante team) have been helping me decide on what helps me through life, and decide what can make me happy . . . instead of just working to work."

With high motivation and aspirations came deep concerns about how they would pay for college and the strain it would place on their family. Perhaps Monica said it best when she said,

> School is expensive; you try your best to do good things in high school so that you can get scholarships, but sometimes it's not good enough, and you still have to pay for your college. It's kind of nerve-wracking.

Though financial struggles were a concern, they also served as a motivating factor for these 8th-graders. Unlike youth from more affluent families, their reasons for wanting to go to college often included their family and not wanting to struggle economically. Throughout our pláticas, the students expressed this via multiple comments, such as the following:

I want to have a good career so I can help my mom and stuff. (Jessica)

Most of my cousins from my family, they all dropped out of high school except for one cousin. I want to motivate my little cousins to get into college. (Berta)

I want a better future for me. Not to be the person who works in McDonald's, like a fast-food place and struggles to pay their bills. (Kati)

For me it is important to go to college for myself because when I grow up I want to be someone. If I have kids, I'm going to tell them that I went to a university. If I went to the university and became a doctor or something, it would be a better life for them. (Bradley)

What is unmistakable from the pláticas with L@s Primer@s is that these young people aspire to go to college and that they understand the economic challenges as well as the benefits of becoming a first-generation college student. They all clearly attributed their early knowledge of college to their experiences in Adelante and have memories of many of those experiences. But in addition to providing these insights, Adelante allowed students to have a racial realist understanding of the systemic inequities they were up against and gave them experiences (such as visiting the university, engaging with undergraduate mentors, and affirming cultural identities) that might help them navigate the oppressive structures and policies that lie before them.

We find hope in the transformative ruptures of L@s Primer@s that has them talking about their dreams to go to college, envisioning themselves in college, or articulating the knowledge they have about college. However, the 10-year Adelante journey has been far from seamless, and the results have been quite mixed in terms of measurable changes in educational policies, school practices, and academic outcomes. In the final section of this chapter, we move from the transformative ruptures and celebratory words of L@s Primer@s to examples of the deep challenges encountered in attempting to disrupt an educational system that was not meant to ensure the academic success of Chican@Latin@ students.

ACADEMIC OUTCOMES AND A CONTINUED TREND OF EXCLUSION

Notwithstanding what L@s Primer@s told us via our pláticas months before they started high school, we witnessed a very slow and uneven change in the school culture and a trend of exclusion that is common for Chican@Latin@ students across the country. Before addressing that trend, we briefly address academic outcomes via standardized test scores that have become a predominant benchmark of academic excellence. Though test scores show positive results for L@s Primer@s, we argue that these scores fail to fully capture Adelante's impact on the students or the school. For example, we looked at test score data[8] for the 2010–2011 academic year. In this year, L@s Primer@s were in 5th grade and most had been participating in Adelante and the dual-immersion program for 6 years. Based on the Criterion-Referenced Test, their collective level of proficiency in language arts was 86%, math 100%, and science 91%. These levels of proficiency were extremely high when compared to those of 5th-graders in a nearby Title I non-dual-immersion school. Although L@s Primer@s' level of proficiency was exciting to us, we note that they were part of the dual-immersion strand and, throughout the school, students in the dual-immersion strand usually had higher overall levels of proficiency than the students in the English-only strand. This, of course, aligns with the dual-immersion research that shows the success of such programs, especially for English language learners (Collier & Thomas, 2004; Freire, 2016). In addition, the mobility rate within the dual-immersion strand was lower than the mobility rate at the neighboring school or in the English-only strand at Jackson. We know that this might also impact test scores. For this reason, we looked at the dual-immersion 6th-grade class at Jackson as another comparison group. This group of students was 1 year ahead of L@s Primer@s and had very limited exposure to Adelante. The 6th-grade comparison group's levels of proficiency on the same exams in the same year were much lower than L@s Primer@s', at 55% in language arts, 61% in math, and 45% in science. Though L@s Primer@s' scores are noteworthy and worth celebrating, we know that test scores only provide part of the picture of academic performance during one snapshot in time.

Moving beyond test scores, we also looked at L@s Primer@s' access to and participation in academically rigorous programs after Jackson. On this measure, they again fared better than the comparison 6th-grade class 1 year ahead of them that did not participate in Adelante, but not as well as students from more affluent Eastside schools. However, the opportunity to access these academically rigorous programs necessitated a direct challenge to the district that is worthy of mention here. During L@s Primer@s' 6th-grade year, the district notified 6th-graders throughout the district about informational meetings and exam dates for the district's Extended Learning Program (ELP) and International Baccalaureate (IB) program for incoming middle school and high school students. ELP is an honors program that "seeks to serve those students at the high end of the [academic] range who possess unique gifts and abilities to succeed in an academic setting" (west. slcschools.org/academics/extended-learning-program). The IB program is touted as the district's preeminent high school honors curriculum and has had very high college placement rates for students who participate in the rigorous course schedule. A fast track to the IB program is through its ELP 7th- and 8th-grade program, and students have to test into it during their 6th-grade year.

However, Jackson 6th-grade students were not notified of the informational meeting or testing dates. The notes with this information were never sent home with them. Via our connections at neighboring schools, we became aware that information about the upcoming ELP and IB testing dates was not shared at Jackson. With great frustration, we contacted the school to find out how and why the Jackson community had not been notified of this opportunity for their students. The response was prompt, apologetic, and assumed responsibility for an "internal glitch." We were assured that information would be sent to parents immediately. Employing a transa, a way of assessing and strategizing against racialized, gendered, and colonial landscapes (Urrieta, 2009), we knew that simply notifying the Jackson parents at such a late date was not enough, so we went a step further and also contacted the district. Below is a portion of a much longer 2011 email to district administrators that was meant to prompt immediate action and remind the district how this was just another example of a long history of exclusion:

> We would like to reiterate our extreme concern for the district's process for notifying parents, the lack of optional programs on the Westside, and what appears to be (at least from our standpoint) a blatant disregard for the parents and students like those we work with at Jackson. Even as we review the information that was sent out on Friday (a day after other 6th-grade parents were able to sit through an hour-long PowerPoint informational meeting), we are completely astounded by district leadership's failure. . . . Why isn't the Jackson community and its students considered a viable partner in continuing educational excellence . . . ? It is clear to us that students and parents on the Westside are once again being excluded systematically, not only because we were not told of this meeting and have not been provided equal access to the test, but because the district is adhering to a long historical pattern of tracking some students into ELP programs and relegating others to regular programs.

The response from the district administrators was slow. In fact, we had to resend the full email, copying two assistant superintendents, including one who has been extremely supportive of Adelante for years. The two administrators then agreed to a meeting to try to remedy the immediate situation. Initially, we were told that Enrique's daughter and Dolores's son could make up the test if they had missed it. This, of course, was unacceptable. They offered other (unacceptable) solutions, and after much negotiation, we all agreed that a short-term solution would be to hold a bilingual informational PowerPoint presentation at Jackson and encourage all 6th-grade families to attend and also schedule an ELP test at Jackson exclusively for all Jackson 6th-graders.

After having to fight for access, 35% of L@s Primer@s participated in an ELP program during their 7th-grade year. Although those results are wonderful, they are also bittersweet because only 6% of the Jackson class 1 year ahead of them participated in an ELP program in 7th grade. In fact, the ELP program has had a long history of excluding students of color and, during the decade we write about, the district was the subject of Federal Office of Civil Rights violations. L@s Primer@s confirmed this continuing pattern of exclusion from academically rigorous programs when a few of them shared with us that during freshman enrollment, high school counselors geared them toward non–college track or "easier" courses. Some of the students felt like "They kind of just wanted us to sign up for whatever and just be finished with it." Genoveva said, "The counselors, they told us that you should probably take earth science, but then our science teacher said that earth science is a waste of time and you should take biology." Quetzal explained that there was a form for students signing up for regular classes and a form for students signing up for the honors classes that were a prerequisite for the IB program. He had the form for the honors classes, but the counselor told him he had the wrong form: "They didn't believe me at first. They didn't think I was going to. . . . They thought I got the wrong paper. She kept telling me it was the wrong one. I just kept telling her." She finally let him sign up for the college track courses, but sadly, these experiences were similar for several of L@s Primer@s, and for countless other Chican@Latin@ students across the country when enrolling in their freshman year of high school.

An understanding of racial realism has helped us confront educational realities such as the IB incident and the recollections about high school enrollment. These two examples demonstrate the presence of deep institutional racism, the myth of meritocracy, and how despite the years of collective work by many partners and the investment in mentors, field trips, oral history activities, parental engagement, the community garden, science camps, ballet folklórico, and so much more, some things have remained the same. Policies and practices reflect the fact that society, educational leaders, and many teachers often do not see Brown kids as college bound. So at best, educational leaders forget about Chican@Latin@ students or, at worst, actively support a system that excludes them. With a significant district achievement gap (Alemán & Rorrer, 2006), the culture of the district has been for many years one that does not include a college-going ethos for Chican@sLatin@s and other students of color. It continues to take much work, many people, and great persistence to disrupt this culture. It often feels as though our 10-year journey has been one in which we take two steps forward and one step back. In the next chapter, we look at the difficulties and challenges of creating a college-going culture by addressing both the choques and transformative ruptures with teachers, educational leaders, and parents.

CHAPTER FOUR

PARENTS, TEACHERS, AND TRANSFORMATIVE RUPTURES

The coming together of two self-consistent but habitually incompatible frames of reference causes un choque. . . .

—Anzaldúa, 1987, p. 78

The 2011–2012 academic year, our seventh year of developing Adelante and working in Jackson, turned out to be our most chaotic and complicated. Throughout the year, a series of choques—ever increasing in their intensity and public nature—threatened Adelante's survival. Collisions within the school, among teachers, and across the community manifested themselves as frustration and anger. Fear among some vulnerable families resulted in a fracturing of school–community relationships. Once informational and informal, parent meetings became tense and turned personal. Although we had forged productive and positive relationships with individual teachers, the faculty became stridently divided on issues related to academic programs and curriculum, parent involvement in the school, and in essence, the role and influence that Adelante had in the school's daily operation. In addition to the IB incident discussed in the previous chapter, a proposed scaling back of the dual-immersion program, along with several administrative decisions, added to the discontinuity and instability in the school. The choques of mindsets and of school direction and purpose among important partners—parents, teachers, and administrators—resulted in "habitually incompatible frames of reference" throughout the year.

In this chapter, we elaborate on both subtle and more overt choques that happened and how they often initiated nepantla—an uncomfortable space of contradiction, dissonance, and transition. Because nepantla is also a space of possibility, we reframe the challenges, conflicts, tensions, and struggles as the spaces and moments where transformative ruptures occurred. We do this first by describing the parent engagement component of Adelante and the ways in which confianza, engagement, advocacy, and leadership had been

48

cultivated with parents. Then, we name the omnipresent choque between asset-based and deficit-based approaches to educating Chican@Latin@ students. Turning to a more overt choque based on a negative school climate, we describe the parent agency, leadership, and activism that emerged as a transformative rupture to the surveillance of Brown bodies in school. Finally, we end with a transformative rupture that opened up the possibility of building bridges between seemingly incompatible frames of reference: deficit thinking and Adelante's pursuit of its social justice principles.

CULTIVATING CONFIANZA, ENGAGEMENT, AND LEADERSHIP

As in other communities of color, support among Jackson parents for college awareness and enrichment activities for their children was never a hard sale to make. Parents consistently committed their time and energy to Adelante and the partnership made efforts to dedicate resources so that parents and family members could attend events. For example, knowing that building confianza among parents, between teachers and parents, and between parents and the Adelante team could lead to the development of emerging leaders and advocates for change, parents were always invited to participate in university field trips. During one of the first field trips, the school bus was filled to capacity. The excitement exhibited by the students and their family members was contagious as children and their family members sang songs on the way to the university. One Latino father mentioned how he had worked all night and, rather than go home to sleep, decided to attend the field trip after working the midnight shift. "I wanted to be here. It's important for her to see me here," he stated during the walking tour of the campus. Another father, an African American maintenance worker employed by the university, surprised his daughter by showing up for the field trip. "My dad works here at the university," the student declared with happiness. As years went on, parents and family members became more comfortable on the university campus. They asked questions about financial aid, housing, and academic preparation, and in essence, they became models of active learning for their children.

This early relationship building and confianza that emerged with parents and family members seemed natural to us. In truth, it was, as some have described, "low-hanging fruit," in that parents were hungry for opportunities for their children. We did not have to teach or tell them how to have high expectations for their children. In fact, these expectations were evident in their high levels of participation in the Adelante programming and were exemplified by the consistent questioning of our long-term commitment to the school and partnership goals: "Will you continue to work with them every year? Will you provide these opportunities when they go to middle school?" Leveraging their support and building on their questions, we initiated community conversations during the first year of the partnership. Inviting parents to engage in pláticas in the neighborhood library, we listened to questions they posed and concerns they shared about immigration, under- and unemployment, health care, and inadequate or expensive housing. Though they unequivocally supported college awareness and college-preparatory programming, parents also communicated that supporting and sustaining their families during the economic downturn was an issue they wanted to discuss. These early pláticas signaled a developing confianza and set the foundation for parent advocacy, and they also reminded us to always consider the macro-political and societal factors that impacted students and their families on a daily basis.

When we first entered the school, we noticed that school staff sought to engage parents and families in traditional ways. The school held a Segunda taza de café/Second Cup of Coffee event once a month that was meant to be a kind of social hour for parents. School information was shared, parent concerns were discussed (at least on a surface level), and topics such as tips for "parenting successfully" were sometimes presented. Although we are not discounting the utility of spaces like the Segunda taza de café/Second Cup of Coffee, our goal was broader in that we wanted to engage parents with discussions about their everyday concerns, provide them with resources to be advocates for their children, and create spaces for a discourse of college expectation to occur. So, in the spring of 2009, Adelante developed and implemented its first Community Advocate Program for parents with a series of Saturday workshops.[1] Childcare and food were provided, and parents received a stipend after completing the workshops. The workshop series continued for a couple of years and was a huge investment in time, energy, and human resources, but the workshops were responsive to parents' requests for information and resources related to domestic violence, immigration laws, legal services, childhood obesity, sex education for children, and parental rights in schools.

By the fall of 2013, a core group of parents, almost exclusively mothers, had become active in different ways in the school. Some of the mothers, who had initially participated as members of the Segunda taza de café/Second Cup of Coffee and the Community Advocate Program, had coalesced into an active Padres en acción/Parents in Action group. Although our graduate students helped access resources and facilitate dialogues, they consistently removed themselves from any of the decision making and promoted the idea of group facilitation, agenda setting, and event planning.[2] Parent leaders addressed a range of issues and planned activities related to Dia de Los Niños/Day of the Children, parent–teacher zumba classes, Jackson's first community garden, parent–teacher dialogues, and teacher appreciation events. In the decade we write about, the process of moving from engagement to community advocacy to emergent leadership was strategically cultivated.

DEFICIT DISCOURSES AS THE ONGOING OMNIPRESENT CHOQUE

I think they [my students] should learn how to do something with their hands. You know, fix cars or whatever. That [they should choose] something that they love to do and can do and will help them make money [long pause]. College takes a lot of brainpower, you know, and sometimes there isn't that brainpower in all students.

—Jackson teacher

Although we have spent much time cultivating confianza with parents and facilitating spaces for their advocacy and emergent leadership and activism, our relationship building with teachers has always been less developed. This is not to say that we have not had successes and authentic and productive relationships with teachers and leaders in the school—we have. However, the most challenging aspect of our development of Adelante has been in building widespread relationships between teachers and members of the Adelante team. This inability has prevented more and deeper levels of collaboration. The epistemologically divergent perspectives on Chican@Latin@ educational needs contributed to what we think of as an ever-present choque between the deficit discourses, like the quote above, and the asset-based discourses and social justice principles of Adelante. It is important for us to acknowledge that the social justice principles that the partnership was founded upon were not co-constructed with the school staff. Rather, we, as parents and scholar activists, brought the principles to the center of all that we did—our selection of the site, the recruitment of graduate students as part of the Adelante team, development and implementation of programs, and engagement with members of this community. So, Adelante's foundational core and our approach to working with students and families as holders and creators of knowledge collided with the deficit thinking of many of the teachers.

Deficit discourses and practices often persist in the professional lives of educators and permeate school buildings across the country (García &

Guerra, 2004; Solórzano & Yosso, 2001b). Jackson is no different. In the decade we spent building the partnership, deficit thinking has been ubiquitous. For example, since the first year of the partnership, college student mentors have disclosed how they do not know what to do with the deficit comments teachers make to students. Some of the mentors analyzed these deficit discourses in their service learning reflections using the critical readings from their college course, but they usually felt helpless to interrupt them as they occurred. Parents also shared how frustrated they felt when teachers said or did things that did not value the students' home language or culture. In both of these examples, undergraduate students and parents described and shared the majoritarian stories that dominate and shape perceptions about Chican@Latin@ students, families, and the communities in which they live (Alemán, 2009b; Valencia & Black, 2002; Yosso, 2006).

We understand this collision of mindsets as an ongoing omnipresent choque that is based on vastly different ways of thinking about the Jackson students and their families. It is important to note that not all teachers voiced deficit-based discourses, and a few of the 25 teachers at Jackson regularly shared ideas and discourses that aligned more closely with the tenets of social justice or culturally relevant educators. Those teachers did not describe parents or students as lacking knowledge or as devaluing education. Instead, they made statements like "[My] students are pretty motivated kids. . . . They have a lot of stuff going on. There's lots of poverty. . . . But I think they're pretty motivated." However, these discourses were less common than the comments we report below from teacher interviews that took place in the fall of 2011.[3]

For example, there were teachers who had decided that some of their elementary students—even as young as kindergarten—lacked the intellectual skill or ability to go to college. One teacher stated that college is just "not for everyone." Another teacher pointed to how, growing up, she personally was always expected to go to the University of Utah, and there was no other choice after high school. However, in reference to her own students, she held much lower expectations:

> I would love my students to do well in school, to love coming to school, to want to learn more and more, to continue on into 7th grade (chuckles), let alone 9th grade (chuckles). And if they could go to college, that would be wonderful. I'd love to have them all go to college. But I don't know for sure if that's going to work out for them, . . . Well, money, family issues, and I think some kids just shouldn't go to college.

Deficit thinking regarding students' ability to attend college or to achieve at high levels was displayed when some educators explained that students would have limited college access because parents lacked the education, the appropriate culture, and/or the ability to make appropriate decisions for their children. One teacher specifically argued that lack of educational priorities was the reason parents were not involved in the school. She stated:

> They're, they just sort of stay, they live in their own little worlds. They don't have enough money to do much of anything. But they do always go back to Mexico, sometimes for Christmas, and they do go to California. So they travel home to see family a lot. Not as much as they used to, but they still do.

Despite the school having one of the district's few dual-immersion programs, another teacher blamed parents' "language barriers" and believed parents lacked the skills and know-how to participate in their children's education. She stated:

> I do think that the language barrier does make things really hard and so that is one thing that is lacking and the culture just in the environment, just trying to get parents comfortable to come into the classroom.

Finally, another teacher explained that home culture and parenting skills were sometimes lacking. Although she praised her current students, she described how "manners" sometimes had to be learned in school. She stated:

> I'm lucky because most of my students do have like, I guess, sometimes I might call it, you know, good home training, manners. And if they don't have that, I hope that they can kind of learn that in school so they know how to treat people.

Research demonstrates that many White, middle-class teachers—not just the teachers at Jackson—are unprepared by teacher education programs to work with students from low socioeconomic backgrounds and/or historically marginalized student populations (García & Guerra, 2004). Few teacher education programs prepare teachers to effectively cross into their students' worlds. Nor do many teacher education programs give teachers the tools to deconstruct deficit views and teach "against the grain" via social justice or culturally relevant teaching orientations (Cochran-Smith, 1991; 2004).

The deficit-based discourses at Jackson, which viewed students and parents as lacking, collided with the contrasting asset-based discourses of Adelante. This omnipresent choque provides the backdrop for many of the fractures and tensions that have been present, as well as the more visible and overt choque that we discuss next.

FRUSTRATION, SURVEILLANCE, AND THE DISCIPLINING OF BROWN STUDENTS

While working with teachers and attempting to counter the deficit-minded discourses and practices exemplified above, many Jackson families were also living under constant fear of surveillance and deportation. Utah state legislation barring the issuance of driver's licenses to non-U.S. residents and the elimination of in-state tuition for undocumented high school graduates were introduced and debated annually since 2005. The rise of national ideologues such as Governor Jan Brewer of Arizona, Kris Kobach of Kansas, and most recently, Donald Trump, has further exacerbated the anti-immigrant and xenophobic sentiment that families and their children were forced to contend with. Although we participated in immigrants' rights marches with Jackson families, sponsored pláticas to communicate information to immigrant families when new state and federal legislation was proposed, and wrote letters of support for family members who were fighting for their status in the legal system, the anti-immigrant policy and legal choques that were thrust upon families and youth in the Jackson community were constant. In the midst of this societal tumult, the following example from the Jackson community informs our understanding of how a public, school-level choque can both destabilize relationships and reaffirm the need for partnership work.

Whether it was an early fall day with the bright yellow leaves on the aspens marking the changing of the seasons or a late winter day when most of the school's surrounding soccer fields are covered with snow, the asphalt play areas encircling the school always teemed with activity and energy. During recess, basketball, soccer, hopscotch, and tag all signaled students' exuberance as they played, a necessity for the release of energy built up during the school day. Yet, it was during a particularly warm late spring when students were made to sit on the hot asphalt—in what teachers called a "time-out square"—that a visible and intense choque was triggered. When parents became aware of the practice, they were frustrated, confused, and angered.

In several meetings organized by the parents to mobilize against this harsh policy, they often expressed their concern with tears and anger. Several lamented the timeout square tactic used by teachers and questioned,

"Por qué no se los ponen en la sombra, bajo un árbol, no en el calor del sol, no en el cemento caliente?" ("Why don't they put them in the shade, under a tree, not in the hot sun, not on the hot cement?") Despite parents having spoken to school officials and receiving what they felt were assurances that it would not occur anymore, the practice of putting students deemed unruly or in need of discipline in a hot timeout square continued. Parents pointed to this practice as one of many that created "un clima negativo" ("a negative school climate") for their families, including policies such as parents not being allowed in the halls when dropping off their children in the morning, a "tardy table" at lunch for students who were late to school, and teachers who did not allow students to go to the bathroom during class. During one meeting, suggestions for more appropriate discipline practices were offered by the parent attendees. It was clear that parents did not resist discipline for their children. In fact, they expected respectful children–niños educa- dos–but they also demanded that the school respect the children back. One mother stated, "No estamos diciendo que no castiguen. Si ellos no están escuchando la maestra, pues disciplinen de manera apropiada." ("We're not saying not to punish them. If they are not listening to the teacher, then dis- cipline them appropriately.")

The negative climate parents experienced came to a head in late spring when a few mothers exiting the school witnessed the child of one of the mothers who played an active role in mobilizing their efforts sitting in a timeout square under a hot sun. When the parents informed the mother that her child was being disciplined in this way, it triggered a very public choque. Parents renewed their organizational efforts and decided to take their con- cerns that were not being addressed by the school to the district office. They requested that we–Enrique and Dolores–accompany them to the district.

The very next day, mothers met in the school parking lot after dropping off their children. Not all the mothers had access to their own car, so several Adelante team members volunteered to drive. At the district office, every- one took the stairs up to the third floor and walked into a small office where an administrative assistant asked what she could do to help us. Dolores was explaining the group's request for a meeting when an older White female administrator, who had been working for the district for almost 30 years, walked out of her office. The assistant pointed to the group and said, "This group is here to talk to you." The administrator appeared to be taken aback by such a large group of Brown female bodies in her office and, without ad- dressing the parents, quickly stated, "I don't have time to meet with anyone today. In fact, I have a meeting in a few minutes. They can't just come in here and expect to meet with me." Neri Oliva, our graduate student who was translating for the mothers, was told in Spanish by one of the mothers,

"Tell her that we are here to discuss serious issues and concerns." Neri communicated this to the administrator who, again without really addressing the parents, abruptly replied, "I understand, but they can't just come in and expect to be able to talk to me. They need to schedule an appointment first."

Although we wanted to respond directly to her disrespect toward the group of mothers, we kept the interests of the mothers as our priority and relied on a spontaneous transa to respond to the racialized and gendered landscape. So, when the administrator (again without acknowledging the mothers) motioned the two of us to step into her office to propose a meeting, we obliged. However, deliberately leaving the administrator waiting, after the administrator suggested a date, Dolores stepped back out of the office to see if the day and time worked for the mothers. Once the meeting was confirmed, the administrator walked past the group of mothers without saying anything to them.

As the administrator exited, Mrs. Hanson, a district leader of color who has been a strong ally, entered from a back hallway. She greeted all the mothers, and Enrique briefly told her why they were there and that the administrator they came to see could not meet with the parents today. Mrs. Hanson quickly invited the parents to a very small conference room down the hall, apologizing that she didn't have a larger space in which to meet at the moment. Neri translated Spanish to English and English to Spanish. During an hour-long meeting, Mrs. Hanson listened, asked questions, and took notes as the parents expressed their concerns and explained why they had come to the district office. Mrs. Hanson made no promises and took no immediate action, but she expressed sincere concern and informed the parents that she would be present at the meeting in 2 days. As we exited the small conference room, the parents all thanked her and each of them shook her hand good-bye.

As we walked outside the building, the mothers started speaking, and one of the mothers asked, "Pues, que vamos hacer ahora?" ("So what are we going to do now?") We all stopped to talk outside the main entrance. Responding to the question, but also speaking to the rest of the group, another mother said, "Todos vamos a asistir a la reunión. Tenemos dos días más para notificar a los padres acerca la reunión. Esperemos que más padres puedan venir." ("We are all going to come to the meeting. We have two days to notify more parents about the meeting. Hopefully, more parents can come.") The mothers nodded in agreement, and a third, often very quiet mother suggested, "Podemos pedir a aquellos que no pueden asistir a la reunión para escribir una carta indicando sus preocupaciones y experiencias en la escuela." ("We can ask those that can't come to the meeting to write a letter stating their concerns and experiences at the school.") Some offered to begin making phone calls to other parents and someone else suggested that each of them should talk to parents and families as they picked up their kids from school. Before walking to the cars, the mothers confirmed their action plan to prepare for their meeting.

The choque that resulted from the timeout square policy and un clima negativo is one example–a very visible and destabilizing example–of the extent to which choques occurred within Adelante not only during this particular year, but in partnership work more generally. Although tensions within the school among teachers, administrators, families, and the Adelante team had simmered, built up, and been ignored for some time, this choque initiated a state of nepantla that was chaotic, painful, and difficult for everyone to maneuver. Some teachers were quietly supportive of the parents' actions; others were angry that parents had gone to the district; and some believed we had personally initiated this move. However, our transa was to follow the mothers' leadership and support them in the ways we could, such as providing transportation, translation, or our positional authority as university faculty when talking with district officials. Some families wanted to distance themselves from the mothers who went to the district, and others were frightened about possible repercussions. Things continued to escalate, especially when district security was sent to one immigrant mother's home after a verbal altercation between her and school officials. However, in the midst of the pain and anguish of this nepantla that lasted through the end of the semester and into the next academic year, parent leadership emerged, community members were energized and motivated to continue forward, and teacher allies continued to look for ways to implement partnership activities in their classrooms. We attempted to utilize our positionalities as faculty members, U.S. citizens, and educational scholars to stress community arguments at the district office, in School Community Council meetings, and in discussions with teachers and school leadership. But we understand the parent leadership, and more specifically, the mother leadership, as the transformative rupture that allowed individual and group agency, leadership, activism, and coalitional creativity to emerge.

Because at the time the pain itself was difficult to witness and work through, it was not easy to imagine the possibilities for transformation in school practices and policies. The choque between mindsets about how to treat Brown youth and how to engage Brown families was evident in the very real divide within the school community, and also within the mothers' initial encounter at the district. Though our racial realist framework guided our understanding of these divides and the events that took place, the immediate anger and frustration that resulted prevented us from seeing the transformative ruptures. It was not until we could look back in hindsight that we realized that the daily choques faced in partnership work can, in fact, lead to transformative ruptures—those moments and incidents of possibility when unjust policies, practices, or discourses can be challenged, disrupted, and destabilized.

(RE)BUILDING ALLIES FROM A TRANSFORMATIVE RUPTURE

When we returned from summer break, the air was still thick with unease, distrust, and apprehension among parents, teachers, students, and the Adelante team. After the turmoil around the discipline policy and the parents' advocacy at the district, yet another leader was assigned to the school. She and the social-justice oriented vice principal were both very supportive of strengthening Adelante's goals and programs and rebuilding relations between parents and teachers. The timeout square discipline policy had ended, as had the tardy table and the rule that parents could not walk the halls in the morning when dropping off their children. Many teachers recommitted to the idea of increased communication with the Adelante team and expressed their desire to have their voices heard and be part of conversations regarding Adelante. The teachers completed an equity survey that was initiated by the District Equity Office and disseminated by the school-based equity team. Teachers' feedback stated that they wanted (1) time to learn from others' experiences, (2) time to self-reflect, and (3) time to discuss equity topics with colleagues.

In response to their desire to increase communication with Adelante and the feedback from the equity survey, the Adelante team, with support from the school leadership, began to develop regular structured conversations with the faculty at Jackson. School leadership scheduled monthly professional development time during faculty meetings for the Adelante team and teachers to engage one another—a transformative rupture to the limited access we previously had to formally engage with teachers outside of the classroom.[4] During these meetings there was food and facilitated dialogues on topics such as culturally relevant pedagogy, best practices with college student mentors, and transforming deficit discourses. We viewed the teachers' desire to have increased conversations on equity topics and the principal's commitment to making sure these conversations happened as a positive sign—a transformative rupture from previous years and first steps in (re)building relationships.

A specific example of the transformative rupture in which we saw the possibility of bridging the divide between nos/otras and the seemingly incompatible frames of reference took place at one of these faculty meetings.

The meeting occurred in Jackson's library, with nearly all the teachers seated around large worktables that had been moved around to accommodate a face-to-face planned dialogue. Employing a transa to more effectively steer faculty conversations toward social justice, we strategically asked a White graduate student, former classroom teacher, and ally who had been collaborating with us to prepare and facilitate a professional development workshop. We knew that teachers would be more open to having a tough discussion about race with a White woman from outside of Adelante than with either of us. Our goal was to talk about equity issues and deficit discourses by listening to and learning from the experiences of the college student mentors. The graduate student ally masterfully led the discussion through uncomfortable silences and tense sharing.

More specifically, Jackson teachers collectively spent time watching digital stories that were the educational journeys of college students of color who had been mentoring at Jackson all year. These autobiographical narratives pointed to the challenges in their educational journeys as first-generation college students, including being placed in lower-track courses and having K–12 teachers who had held low expectations of them. The digital stories were powerful and created a bridge that allowed the teachers to learn from experiences that were very different from their own: a bridge that brought "us" and "them" closer to a collective nos/otras. Asked to spend time reflecting on the narratives, most teachers seemed genuinely moved by the stories of these college students. Teachers then moved to collectively thinking and talking about what it means if some teachers believe a college-going culture is too lofty of a goal for Jackson students. Many of the deficit quotes from teachers that were presented earlier in this chapter were shared. There were teachers who did not believe that the deficit quotes were from Jackson teachers, others who bravely confronted their own biases, and still others who appeared not to be surprised by the quotes from their colleagues.

Though it was a difficult discussion about how low academic expectations shape the educational journey of students of color, it was certainly a small step in the right direction. Our transa to confront the deficit ideologies with a White ally and the powerful stories of undergraduate mentors of color allowed us to take a small step in bridging vastly different perspectives on the schooling of Brown students. This strategy was not without risk, but it resulted in a transformative rupture to deficit thinking and to the nos/otras or the "us versus them" mentality that had been so prevalent since the previous year. In the next chapter, we expand on our discussion of Adelante's college student mentors, their powerful narratives, and their shifting identities.

CHAPTER FIVE

Politicizing Diversity Scholars in a White University

> They [the Jackson students] remind me of why I'm in school and why it's important for me to stay in school. They motivate me to keep going when sometimes I get burned out with school, work. . . . I guess that's the important thing about the mentor/mentee relationship is that both are better because of the experience and benefit and learn from each other. Being a mentor allows me to collaborate with students, teachers . . . as well as provides the opportunity to give back to the community that has given me so much. Being a first-generation student of color myself, I am aware of the struggles that the students will face in education. Having come from a very similar background, I know how critical Adelante is to children at Jackson Elementary and have been honored to be part of the program.
>
> —Shari, 2006–2007 mentor

Shari's words echo many of the nearly 700 undergraduate mentors of color who between 2005 and 2015 spent 1 hour, once a week, for 1 academic year, mentoring elementary school students at Jackson Elementary as part of the Adelante program. Several scholars note that mentoring relationships can act as a form of academic support and a retention strategy for undergraduate students, where the undergraduate student is the mentee and the mentoring experience is a one-way endeavor primarily benefiting the mentee (Jacobi, 1991; Walker & Taub, 2001). However, in speaking about her experience as a mentor, not a mentee, Shari points to how her role as a mentor to Jackson students contributed to her own college retention. In initiating the mentoring component of the Adelante partnership, we sought to contribute positively to the educational experience of elementary school students as mentees, not completely realizing how deeply university students would benefit as mentors. In previous chapters, we addressed how the presence of the mentors' bodies allowed Jackson students to see themselves in their mentors and allowed Jackson teachers to (re)imagine different futures for their own students. However, what also became clear was the impact that mentoring had on undergraduates like Shari in the form of ethnic/racial affirmation, engagement on campus, rates of retention, and being empowered to talk back to dominant discourses.

In order to recount the story of this impact, we first have to share the evolution of the University of Utah's Diversity Scholars Program, a first-year academic support and retention program for college students of color that also provides service learning opportunities to mentor younger students participating in Adelante or in other service learning sites. The first half of this chapter outlines the creation and development of the Diversity Scholars Program, including its key players and essential allies; the majoritarian discourses that the program challenged; and its relationship to the university's Ethnic Studies Program, Adelante, and other campus units. We document the development of the Diversity Scholars Program because it demonstrates how the mentoring component of Adelante has become institutionalized. We also do so because, as we will demonstrate, the Diversity Scholars Program illustrates a transformative rupture to a predominantly White institution (PWI). In the second half of the chapter, we analyze how the mentors make sense of their experiences mentoring at Jackson and participating in the Diversity Scholars Program. We use Anzaldúa's concept of nepantla to explain the way the mentors understood their shifting identities and the concept of transformative ruptures to describe their ability to think critically about societal inequities and to talk back to dominant discourses.

PROGRAM DEVELOPMENT AS A TRANSFORMATIVE RUPTURE

Initially in 2005, Adelante secured approximately 20 mentors from the University of Utah's chapter of MEChA (Movimiento Estudiantil Chican@ de Aztlán), a longstanding national Chican@ student organization and a handful of mostly graduate students of color from our respective home departments. MEChA's commitment to serve communities of color, and the inclination of the graduate students to work with younger students of color, lent itself to this collaboration. By the end of its second year, Adelante was in need of additional mentors as the program expanded to include Jackson's 1st-graders. As a result, we needed to plan for continued growth with a consistent pipeline of college student of color mentors.

An opportunity arose in 2007 when Dr. Villalpando assumed the position of associate vice president for the Office for Equity and Diversity at the University of Utah. From the onset of his tenure, one of his central goals was to increase the number of students of color on campus and support their retention. He conceptualized a first-year retention program specifically for students of color. Referred to as the Diversity Scholars Program, it was based on critical race theoretical tenets. Supporting students of color throughout their first year on campus, the program required participants to regularly interact with faculty and staff of color, enroll in a yearlong ethnic studies curriculum with strong foundations in critical race theory, receive academic advising from advisors in the Center for Ethnic Student Affairs (CESA),[1] participate in multiple mentoring relationships, and engage with off-campus service learning experiences. Reflecting on his early vision for the Diversity Scholars Program, Dr. Villalpando explained that a retention program housed at CESA predated the Diversity Scholars Program and inspired him to recast it as a fully resourced program rooted in the best practices that had been identified by higher education scholars. He said:

> First there was the Utah Opportunity Scholars, a scholarship program for high-achieving students of color that operated a class to support them in their first year. Separate from that, there was also a one-unit seminar that was offered to students who hadn't met minimum university admission standards and whose admission to the U had been sponsored[2] by CESA. Neither course was taught regularly by faculty, neither course had an academic home, and neither course was connected to the other. Based on my work with similar programs at three previous campuses, and what I knew from the higher education literature on first-year cohort models, learning communities, same-race peer affiliation, and the educational benefits of ethnic studies courses, it was a no-brainer. We needed to create a mixed-ability, freshman cohort model that would politicize students to understand educational inequities, provide a rigorous ethnic studies curriculum, and provide service learning credit for being engaged in communities of color. It needed an academic home. I knew it would require extra work and commitment to get it off the ground, so that's when I reached out to the Ethnic Studies Program and to you two [Enrique and Dolores].

Though it was a "no-brainer" for Dr. Villalpando, he recounted the fierce opposition he received from some senior administrative and academic leaders. One senior academic administrator wondered whether the proposal would lead to admitting more students who did not meet the minimum admissions criteria, and a student affairs officer described the proposal as possibly creating a "ghetto for minority students in classes taught by minority faculty." Dr. Villalpando remembered that one dean complained the proposal would result in tracking "even more unqualified minority students into his college." At one point, a campus staff attorney even questioned whether the proposed program might violate "the affirmative action law passed by the U.S. Supreme Court, since it would be designed to attract minority students." Understanding these discourses, Dr. Villalpando (re)framed the arguments for these opponents and cast the program as a retention tool for an increasingly growing and important student population at the university. Enacting what we see as an administrative transa, he used the institution's traditional understandings of student success, merged it with a strong need for the campus, and aligned it with his goal, which had the interests of students of color at its core. The Diversity Scholars Program kicked off in the fall of 2007.

Sharing Dr. Villalpando's research-informed vision of a retention program for students of color, we knew that a relationship between Adelante and the Diversity Scholars Program could help sustain both Adelante and Diversity Scholars. Thus, we agreed to co-create and co-teach the ethnic studies courses of the Diversity Scholars Program and to work with dedicated CESA staff on program development. Together, we served as instructors for the ethnic studies class for multiple years. The early years of getting the Diversity Scholars Program off the ground were very labor-intensive. At the time, the Ethnic Studies Program was running on a deficit budget and had a good number of untenured junior faculty members. Both senior and junior faculty members were invited to teach the courses. Unfortunately, the majority of faculty did not initially have a vested interest in the Diversity Scholars Program. Teaching in the program meant more work, time, and commitment, so many faculty members declined to take it on. Dr. Villalpando later put financial resources into the program, including a small stipend for faculty members teaching in the program, student credit-hour revenue for the Ethnic Studies Program, and funding for a faculty director to coordinate the group of faculty who co-taught the course.[3] As it became clearer how the Diversity Scholars Program would directly serve the Ethnic Studies Program's mission, and as key allies on the faculty became more aware of how the program would bring in financial resources and increase the number of students who would take additional ethnic studies courses or become ethnic studies majors, the Ethnic Studies Program became a relatively more invested partner with the Diversity Scholars Program.[4] Additional faculty committed to teaching the ethnic studies courses.

Engaging in our own transas, we looked for the fissures within a PWI to purposefully develop relationships with allies throughout the university by strategically providing on-campus presentations about Adelante and the Diversity Scholars Program. Our hope was to ensure that different academic and student affairs units on campus understood how each respective program, as well as their relationship with each other, was integral to the university's mission. We presented to a range of administrative and faculty teams, including the Office of Early Outreach, Undergraduate Advising, University Neighborhood Partners, the Ethnic Studies Program, and the Office of Equity and Diversity. Importantly, these presentations allowed us to build key relationships across campus. Ultimately, these relationships functioned to sustain Adelante because partnerships are partially dependent on how invested stakeholders are in the partnership and whether or not the partnership is viewed as core or tangential to a broader mission (Benson et al., 2007; Harkavy, 1998).

Notably, and perhaps serendipitously, around this same time a university-wide task force of faculty members (including Dolores) and administrators came together to apply for a University Community Engagement classification by the Carnegie Foundation. To receive this classification, an institution is required to provide evidence of multiple types of engagement, such as service learning, outreach, and partnerships. Adelante was in its fifth year and the Diversity Scholars Program was in its third year when the university received the designation in 2010. This designation placed community partnerships, service learning, and engaged scholarship at the core of the university's mission. At this time, it was not uncommon to hear Adelante and Diversity Scholars touted as model programs by multiple senior university leaders. We used this recognition to both programs' advantage, particularly Adelante's, as we were always looking for ways to fund and institutionalize different components of the partnership.

Clearly, numerous factors came into play in the institutionalization of Adelante's mentoring component, but by engaging in transas for growth and sustainability, we were able to connect the role of mentors to the broader missions of the Ethnic Studies Program and the university. In the process, both entities became more invested partners. Whether through strategic moves, relationship building, or a (re)framing of the significance of the program, sustaining the mentorship component of Adelante required that the Diversity Scholars Program not be seen as tangential, but rather that it be understood as central to a broader mission dedicated to improving educational experiences for students of color. Today, a dozen faculty members have co-taught the Diversity Scholars courses. And although none of the original founders of the program has continued to have a direct role in it, the partnership with Adelante continues.[5] Given that university resources have been dedicated annually to improving the educational experiences of students of color in the Diversity Scholar Program and several measurable outcomes point to improved retention of the students of color in the program, we consider the Diversity Scholars Program's continued success a transformative rupture to traditional practices at a PWI that has often neglected the needs of these students. In the next section, we spotlight a different type of transformative rupture that resulted from the development of the Diversity Scholars program. To do this, we map out college student mentors' reflections about how mentoring at Jackson Elementary via Adelante and participating in the Diversity Scholars Program impacted them and, in fact, created transformative ruptures in their own experiences as first-year students at the university.

REFLECTIVE AND ENGAGED STUDENT SCHOLARS: AFFIRMATION AND SHIFTING IDENTITIES

As was mentioned previously, the Diversity Scholars Program included enrollment in two ethnic studies courses during the first and second semester for incoming students of color. The content we developed for the courses sought to examine the social, political, economic, and historical context of schooling for students of color in K–12 and higher education. The courses introduced students to concepts and theories that we hoped would help them better understand the educational experiences and realities of historically underrepresented students and navigate their own educational journey.[6] By employing pedagogy that foregrounded social critique and praxis, we sought to engage students across racial groups through structured opportunities to dialogue about topics such as race, culture, language, immigration, gender, and sexuality and how these intersect with their educational trajectory. One of our goals in assigning readings, facilitating discussions, and creating learning activities was to challenge students to be more reflective about their own educational experiences and the schooling conditions of students of color in general. Another, less explicit goal (not listed on the syllabi) had to do with nurturing self-love via ethnic/racial affirmation by providing students with the analytical tools to gain strength from typically marginalized identities. In a sense, the curriculum provided them with the analytical and navigational tools to develop and enact their own transas as first-year students, navigating a PWI. In requiring a yearlong, service learning experience mentoring Chican@Latin@ and other youth of color, we encouraged students to apply the discourses from class to their mentoring experiences, their lives on campus, and the ongoing public debate over educational (in)equity.[7]

Over the years, the Diversity Scholars have been an extremely diverse group of students.[8] In what follows, we examine how these diverse young people narrate their experiences related to the ethnic studies courses and their yearlong mentoring experience with Adelante.[9] We focus on two of the themes that emerged from our analysis: identities in the making and talking back to dominant discourses.[10] These patterns align with the goals of the curriculum and pedagogy intended for the class and cultivated transformative ruptures in their journey through higher education.

Identities in the Making: The Hyphenated Lives of Undergraduates

Utilizing Anzaldúa's (2002) conceptualization of nepantla, we argue that the first-year ethnic studies courses, coupled with their mentoring experiences at Jackson, often placed the students within nepantla—that liminal space or process where transformation and learning occurred. We use nepantla to make sense of how they reflected on the ongoing construction of their identity and the learning they were engaged in via their mentoring and the ethnic studies courses. For example, Norman (2007–2008 cohort), a self-identified "Hispanic/Caucasian," positioned himself as an outsider to the community where Jackson is located. He described the working-class community of color in deficit terms, stating, "I was kind of nervous at first to do this, and like, it's in . . . not the best area. I didn't like really know a lot about it, just kind of like nervous about what it would be like." Norman grew up in a predominantly White community where he had little connection to other Chican@sLatin@s or to his Latin@ heritage. Yet, when asked how he was similar to or different from the students he mentored, Norman pointed out that he is a first-generation college student, he described how he and the kids he mentored have parents who were not able to go to college, and he reflected on how the kids' stories reminded him of his grandfather's. He expressed a connection with the students, but recognized his White privilege when he stated, "It's nice to have people to relate to and . . . I didn't really have too many people to relate to in that way [growing up]. I'm Caucasian at the same time, so it wasn't as hard as like it might have been for other people."

In a space of nepantla, Norman described the tension he experienced being Latino and White, pushed to the margins in White spaces, but also deriving capital from his Whiteness relative to other Latin@ students. In this nepantla space, Norman felt connected to the elementary students and described examples of how he was able to support them in various ways. He emphasized that his identification as Latino was cultivated by his mentoring experience and through his interactions with the bilingual youth: "These kids are only in kindergarten and they do things I need to be working on.

They know what ethnicity they are and they're not afraid to [show it]." Norman described how he learned to embrace his Latino identity and the Spanish language more openly from the children. Stating that he declared a minor in Spanish as a result of his mentoring experience, he explained that mentoring in Adelante provided him with access to a rich space in which the ongoing construction of his identity as a Latino had been affirmed.

The idea that elementary students influenced the mentors' experiences of cultivating or remaking their own social, political, or ethnic identities is not unique to Norman, or to Chican@Latin@ students. Many mentors shared this experience, including two Native American students, Madeline and Vanessa (2012–2013 cohort), who talked candidly about how mentoring young bilingual Spanish speakers influenced them to start learning their heritage language, deepen their cultural ties to family on the reservation, and contribute to ceremonies. Madeline said that mentoring at Jackson made her want to embrace and maintain her cultural ways: "I see kids speaking their language and it makes me feel shameful that I don't know my language very well." Vanessa added, "Jackson made me realize that I wasn't deeply connected to my Native American roots."

Ester (2007–2008 cohort), a self-identified "Latina immigrant," also expressed shame while reflecting on the painful memories of first coming to this country, having difficulty learning English, and then wishing she were White:

> I can't believe that I wanted to be White. I didn't wanna be myself, I didn't wanna belong in my family. I . . . it makes me angry [her voice begins to crack] now because it's all that pressure of, you know, you have to be, you have to speak English, you have to be White, you have to accommodate. I had to leave my culture behind. I had like two other Latina friends and the rest of my friends were White. [And I felt] like [I] didn't really belong with them or with the Latinos.

Ester and many other students traced the tension that they experienced to a sense of not belonging either here or there. It was within this in-between space of nepantla that she and others took up colonial discourses that oppressed themselves and others. Six months after completing her mentoring and the ethnic studies course, Ester reflected on the colonial discourses she had taken up before entering the class. She said she had been "blinded to a lot of the things that we talked about in class" and that both the mentoring and the course allowed her to reflect on the contradictions in her life, to understand how her identities had been negated, and to wrestle with her performance of a White identity.

Similar to Ester, many of the undergraduate mentors reflected on their struggles with internalizing an oppressive hierarchy that led them to perform a White identity or deny their cultural heritage. For example, in a written narrative that incorporated discourses from the ethnic studies course, Kyung (2012–2013 cohort) discussed the uncomfortable space of nepantla from which he struggled with his Korean American identity as a child and how he wanted to change his Korean name to an American name. He said:

> Whiteness had taken over my brain. . . . All I ever wanted was to fit in and be like a "normal" person in this White community. . . . I was mad at her [his mother] for giving me a weird name that no one even knew how to pronounce. I would ask my mom if we could go get my name legally changed before middle school. . . . I felt like I was dealing with two different identities and I struggled with it. . . . It must've killed my parents when I was "embarrassed" of our culture and when I rebelled against them for it. . . . I wish now that I could've told my younger self to just love yourself and be happy with who you are.

A choque of mindsets, of ways of being, and even of the legitimacy of his name, prompted Kyung to struggle with his Korean and American identities. Similar to the way that mentoring allowed Kyung to reflect on the struggles with his identities, Roxanne (2012–2013 cohort) reflected on how she once distanced herself from her Samoan identity and language. She shared how exposure to critical discourses allowed her to actually embrace that in-between space—the uncomfortable nepantla where cultural and linguistic identities often collide. She used to avoid speaking Samoan, and said, "But then when I came here, and ethnic studies have shown us . . . cultural, oh, what's that word (short pause) uh, yeah, cultural straddler. I want to be like that, like be in-between." Roxanne and Kyung used the discourses from class and their mentoring experiences to destabilize the colonial discourses that support dominant beliefs about language, culture, and belonging. Wilfred (2009–2010 cohort), an African American mentor, also spoke about a destabilization in the performance of his current identity, specifically as a result of mentoring youth at Jackson:

> On my way home I realized that those kids were like a mirror of who I was at their age. They also showed me who I was becoming. Before even meeting them, I thought I was better than them. They opened my eyes and made me realize who I was becoming. I was isolating myself from who I was as a child. Those kids had the same

experiences as I did, the struggles, the goals, and disadvantages that I had. I was doing what my mother always taught us not to do, and that is to forget where I came from and trying to isolate myself from my people.

All of these undergraduate students reflected on their own nepantla. From what they shared, it seems that the process of reinventing and affirming their identities was shaped by their interactions with the elementary school students they mentored, the course material they were exposed to, and the cohort of undergraduate students they interacted with during their first year on campus. The process sometimes put them into a painful space as they reflected on their younger or current selves and the ways in which they had often negated or abandoned parts of who they are. This is because, "[d]uring nepantla, our worldviews and self-identities are shattered. . . . But nepantla is also a time of self-reflection, choice, and potential growth" (Keating, 2006, p. 9). The mentoring experience and the ethnic studies curriculum stimulated the nepantla in which many students found themselves, and in some ways, this liminal space prepared students of color to navigate higher educational environments. In the next section, we see how these spaces of nepantla resulted in transformative ruptures that allowed students to use the new ideas, discourses, and shifting identities to talk back to dominant discourses that frame different forms of oppression.

Talking Back: "It Gave Me Tools I Could Apply"

For the mentors, the ethnic studies cohort courses were almost always the most ethnically/racially diverse classes they took on campus. For most, it was also the first time they were introduced to theories, ideas, and concepts that allowed them to think critically about societal inequities and about how marginalized peoples navigate and work against those inequities. Over and over again, the Diversity Scholars demonstrated the different ways that they used these discourses to, as bell hooks (1989) says, "talk back" to dominant discourses about people of color, women, the marginalized, and the queer. We see their "talking back" as transformative ruptures that disrupt divisive binaries and colonial ways of thinking about language, race, gender, class, and sexuality.

Initially, the readings and class discussions left Rebeca (2007–2008 cohort), a self-identified "immigrant Latina," confused. She, like a few other students, at first wondered if the ideas from class pushed them to engage in a kind of "reverse discrimination." Crediting the readings and discussions with her class peers, she believed she obtained the tools to begin to question her perspectives. Rebeca said she could now "look deeper into a situation. . . . Without the class, I don't think I would have tackled a lot of points that I needed to." She realized that talking about race and racism does not mean one is racist, and that participating in a course with students of color where cross-racial dialogues were facilitated allowed her to see how similar, yet different, their experiences were.

Eduardo (2007–2008 cohort), a self-identified "Chicano Latino Afromestizo Mexican immigrant," talked about making use of the new discourses and cross-racial dialogues to better understand the subjectivities of other communities of color and to build alliances. He described the tense relationship between Pacific Islanders and Chican@sLatin@s in his urban high school, a tension that existed because of a lack of interaction among ethnic groups. The lessons of his body—those he learned via his own Brown body and the Brown bodies of other young people in his school—and the everyday rituals of his high school taught him to not interact with or trust Pacific Islanders. However, these lessons contrasted with the social and discursive space of the ethnic studies course that expected and encouraged cross-racial dialogues. Eduardo felt more equipped to disrupt dominant narratives about other racial/ethnic groups because of the social interactions among students of color and the discourses in class. Giving the example of our discussions of the use of the "N-word" by African Americans and non–African Americans in hip-hop culture and in everyday language, and citing his attendance at a talk given by an African American scholar who provided an in-depth explanation of the historical context for the word, Eduardo said, "I was kind of ignorant. . . . Before you talk about a word, you have to know its history." He went on to be a campus student leader who advocated for the rights of all students of color, undocumented immigrants, and lesbian, gay, bisexual, transgendered, queer communities, and stated that "Respect among [and within] ethnic groups can actually happen," especially if one is able to look beyond divisive binaries to historical and contextual explanations.

Troubling divisive binaries such as male/female, Black/White, good/evil was part of the curriculum. Like Eduardo, Richard (2010–2011 cohort), an African American male student, also used the discourses from class to disrupt binaries that restricted how students of color can imagine who they are. In a group project, Richard, with two other young men of color, decided to send a digital message to high school students of color about how to combat and talk back to stereotypes by disrupting binaries and allowing oneself to exist in that space of nepantla. At one point in the video, Richard states:

If you're an African American, don't think that you have to live by either being what people see you as, by stereotypes, as either some kind of Uncle Tom person, by living in Utah, or by some gangster because of, like, the way you represent yourself. So just be yourself. Live inside the binaries. Be the middle. Just do you.

Applying the critical discourses from the ethnic studies course to the advice they gave younger students or to other courses they took allowed some students to have "more power to . . . talk back to people" and to "feel more confident." During their sophomore year, Chicana students Estrella and Luz (2007–2008 cohort) had a gender studies class that allowed them to integrate and build on the ideas they had already acquired in the Diversity Scholars class. Ester, one of the students who had wished she was White, shared how she was able to use the tools from class to challenge normative ideas in both history and anthropology courses. Although these and other students described the benefits of using these critical discourses in other classes, students also experienced many struggles and difficulties in drawing on the course content to disrupt dominant narratives and colonial ways of thinking about language, race, gender, class, and sexuality. Luz talked about losing friends after she confronted their racist or sexist stereotypes, and Kim (2007–2008 cohort) identified the stress and exhaustion she felt after challenging her professor and the students in her Spanish class regarding their discussion of immigrants: "And it ruined my whole day. I got in a fight with everyone. It's so bad. It's so hard. It's so hard to fight against like 25 people and only me!" Talking back often shifted students into in-between spaces of empowerment and powerlessness, making allies and losing friends, and demonstrating both confidence and insecurity.

In addition to the transformative ruptures to dominant narratives on campus, a few students talked about sharing their new discourses with family. At times, they did this to challenge the colonized or deficit discourses in their homes, and at other times it was to give their own family members the tools to deal with experiences of oppression. Tensions sometimes arose when they used the discourses from class to question the normative constructions of gender, sexuality, and culture or the stereotypes and prejudices they experienced in their own families. Yet, these students felt compelled to share what they were learning with their families. Ester held onto all the readings and made her high school–age sister read some of them. Norman, the mixed-race student who said he learned to embrace his heritage and Spanish language from the youth he mentored, elaborated on the importance of sharing what he learned about race, meritocracy, and privilege with his family, especially the "White side" of his family, who he felt "just doesn't really understand." These conversations were sometimes difficult, as Norman recognized that no one wants to feel like "Oh, I am racist." However, Norman described a transformation in how his family understood these ideas over time and through ongoing discussions. Luz noticed a difference in her mother based on their discussions about what she was learning. Even though Luz's mom characterized some of her new ideas as "crazy," Luz noticed that when her mom talked to others, she would sometimes repeat some of the ideas and even modified the way she thought about particular issues:

> My mom is like, "¡Tú estás loca! Tienes ideas locas." But like sometimes I can see her having conversations with someone else and if they say something that she has heard me talk about . . . she'll start to change her language a little bit . . . she'll start to change a little bit.

Roxanne, whom we earlier indicated had at one time distanced herself from her Samoan identity and language, also talked about teaching new ideas to her family members. She shared that learning about concepts such as microaggressions, resistance, privilege, and racism allowed her to teach them to her family members and, she hopes, her own future children. She said:

> If I were to grow up and get married and have kids, it [knowing these concepts] influences me to like, teach my kids what is right and what is wrong . . . to like be able to speak up about it. . . . I actually taught my brother and my cousin about it. . . . Yeah, and so they'll be like, "Oh my gosh, Roxanne, what's that word again?" And I'm like, "Oh, microaggression." And so he's like, "Oh my gosh, he just totally did that." When I teach it to them, like, they know what's going on. So they know what people are doing.

An overwhelming number of the Diversity Scholars shared the ways in which they, like Roxanne, talked back to dominant narratives found on campus, in society, in their communities, and in their families. Together, the accounts shared above represent the multiple transformative ruptures we have seen in cohort after cohort of Diversity Scholars. Indeed, the Diversity Scholars Program has contributed to a critical mass of students who challenge oppressive discourses and inequitable practices both on and off campus.

THEORY INTO PRACTICE IN THE DIVERSITY SCHOLARS PROGRAM

Driven by critical race feminista praxis, we approached our roles at the university not only as faculty members, but also as activist scholars, "insiders" to the university, and potential conduits to the resources available at a major, research-intensive university. Grounded in advocacy for students of color, our purpose for working with others to codevelop and co-implement the Diversity Scholars Program for first-generation students of color was to cultivate an environment on campus that would facilitate success for students of color. Creating avenues for the university (or units and divisions within the university) to see itself as an invested stakeholder with the Diversity Scholars Program required transas that involved taking a racialized-gendered accounting of the landscape, mapping the resources, developing strategic relationships, and uncompromisingly centering the experiences and needs of college students of color. We described in the first half of this chapter how these types of transas were necessary to initiate, grow, and sustain the Diversity Scholars Program. One can also view its initiation and development as an example of a transformative rupture that does not end Whiteness and institutional racism in higher education, but does chip away at the structural inequities grounded in both of these.

We also understand the relationship between Diversity Scholars and Adelante to be important to sustaining the mentoring component of Adelante. The mentors at Jackson, as we have shown in previous chapters, have been crucial to the goals of Adelante, as they have allowed Jackson students to envision themselves as future college students and have also allowed Jackson teachers to envision their elementary school students as future college students. In this way, the Diversity Scholars Program has been an incubator for transformative ruptures at both a PWI and at an elementary school. In fact, the Diversity Scholars Program demonstrates the cumulative transformative ruptures that can happen to both structures (the school and university) and individuals (the mentors, mentees, and teachers) when students of color have access to high expectations and critical discourses about power, privilege, Whiteness, and marginalized communities.

Looking closely at the mentors, we see that most of them described an uncomfortable space of nepantla in which they reflected on who they were, their relationships to others, and their sense of belonging. Yet their nepantla was also a space of possibility where they were able to use the discourses to critically remap their own educational experiences and shift their identities toward ethnic/racial affirmation and stronger alliances with other students of color. They engaged these critical discourses within the boundaries of their ethnic studies classrooms, but importantly, they also used them within other social spaces and enacted transformative ruptures to dominant colonial discourses. We believe this is a crucial reminder about the need to affirm students' racial/ethnic background, along with other marginalized identities, in ways that allow them to experience self-love and use the strength of their marginalized identities to thrive and disrupt what are often hostile educational climates. This is part of the ethnic/racial affirmation that is at the core of Adelante.

CHAPTER SIX

Consejos for Critical Race Feminista Praxis

In our years coordinating and developing Adelante, we have been invited to present, visit with, learn from, and share information about the partnership with many different types of groups. Whether they are done with faculty, graduate students, parents, undergraduates, state-level policymakers, school district officials, teacher groups, or community organization leaders, our presentations invariably end with audience questions about initiating and sustaining a partnership like Adelante, traversing the tenure and promotion processes while doing this work, or instituting authentic change from within systemically oppressive structures. We have been asked, "How do you manage the day-to-day work with this type of partnership?", "How have you been able to pay for it, grow it, and sustain it for so long?", "How do you work with those who don't buy in to the Partnership goals?", "How do you measure 'success' or keep doing the work when you admittedly can't end institutionalized oppressions in schools?" Our struggle has been not only to describe the complexities of doing this work, but also to respond to these questions comprehensively and with nuance.

In this chapter, we address these and other questions by laying out what we believe are consejos for engaging in critical race feminista praxis. There is much to say about the past 10 years, but limited space requires us to make choices on what we offer. Therefore, our consejos are not all-encompassing, nor are they meant to portray definitive answers to the above questions. Rather, they represent our best attempt to leave readers with "take-aways" for conducting community-based, activist scholarship and to inspire continued work toward anticolonial and antiracist praxis with communities that have been neglected for far too long. Our consejos are organized around three broad, interconnected, and overlapping concepts that we introduced and discussed in the book: nepantla, transas, and transformative ruptures. We begin with nepantla—that liminal middle ground between worlds, identities, and realities—discussing how the concept provides a way for us to understand the messiness of activist research, including the braiding of theoretical orientations, the methodological contradictions that emerge, and the operational and pro-grammatic decisions one is forced to make in developing and sustaining a partnership. Second, we discuss some of our transas, those practical day-to-day negotiations, to provide examples of possible ways to maneuver (or not) within educational institutions. As we talk about transas, nos/otras emerges as one way to make sense of working with the individuals who were key to the partnership, but were not necessarily aligned with the social justice precepts of Adelante. And finally, we return to transformative ruptures and speak about our understanding that triumph (Bell, 1992) can result when spaces for trans-formative ruptures are facilitated and actively promoted for students of color, especially in predominantly White institutions.

NEPANTLA: BEING AT HOME WITH CONFLICT AND AMBIGUITY

As you make your way through life, nepantla itself becomes the place you live in most of the time—home. Nepantla is the site of transformation, the place where different perspectives come into conflict and where you question the basic ideas, tenets, and identities inherited from your family, your education, and your different cultures. Nepantla is the zone between changes where you struggle to find equilibrium. . . .

—Anzaldúa, 2002, p. 548

If we were to return to 2005 to give ourselves consejos about how to ap-proach the development of Adelante, we would start by telling our less ex-perienced selves to be at home in nepantla. In doing this type of work, very little has been straightforward and neat. We realized early on, when choques resulted from various collisions of mindsets, that disagreements, frustrations, and in-between-ness would be the norm. But it took us a while to embrace this state of nepantla as an opportunity for growth, not only in personal and scholarly development, but also in the growth and develop-ment of the partnership. In the midst of creating and sustaining Adelante, the choques and constant state of nepantla actually created spaces for trans-formation for the partnership, just like the mentors' nepantla created a space for transformation in their identities. It was in moments of ambiguity and tension that opportunity to build coalitions emerged. In the decade we write about, we never reached that point where we "got it just right," where all the partnership components ran smoothly without a need for adjustment, where sustainability was a given, or where the school culture was fully asset based and college going. The work was messy, and at times, it was confusing, frustrating, demoralizing, and infuriating. However, at other points in time or at the same time, this work has been uplifting, reaffirming, energizing, hopeful, and spiritual. If we could transport ourselves back to our initial planning meeting with Judith and Octavio, back to the city library, we would tell our past selves that "[n]epantla is, in part, that uneasy feeling of being a part of transformational work" (Alemán, Delgado Bernal, & Mendoza, 2013 p. 336). We should expect conflict and accept the ambiguity because these moments and spaces contain the most potential to unsettle systemic racism and institutionalized oppressions.

One example that illustrates the constant ambiguity and contradiction we experienced is related to the choques between different research priorities, everyday programmatic needs, and the material realities of Jackson community members. These choques led to a methodological nepantla where practice and theory met and often grated against each other and where we questioned our research preparation of graduate students. Our graduate students managed most of the daily operations of Adelante and built relationships with family members, students, and teachers. However, traditional Eurocentric and colonial notions of "what counts" as research in a research-intensive university does not include programming for more than 500 elementary students or building genuine relationships with immigrant families. Striving to limit discussions of priorities like field trips and coordination of undergraduate mentors to 1 hour of our 2-hour weekly team meetings, we were often frustrated with our inability to get all the logistics and coordination done in that amount of time and move on to the "real" research. We knew we were responsible for preparing our students not only to conduct independent research, but ultimately to be prepared and marketable for a faculty career. We worried that the graduate students were spending too much time working with parents, purchasing snacks, or organizing ballet folklórico dance activities, and not enough time reading, thinking, and engaging scholarly literature. In addition, many of the graduate students developed genuine relationships with parents, so they invested time attending family celebrations, sharing life stories, supplying translation services, assisting students outside of school, and providing occasional childcare or rides. Affected by White supremacist and colonial notions of research, we sometimes asked ourselves: Are graduate students engaging too much in the community at the expense of "real" graduate study that is expected of doctoral students at a research-intensive university? Are we doing the students a disservice in their preparation for academic life?

We quelled our misgivings by reassuring ourselves repeatedly that anticolonial research like the critical race feminista praxis we applied is indeed an extremely powerful form of graduate student preparation. It employs critical inquiry, is conducted with marginalized populations, requires reciprocal relationships, and is motivated by "the explicit desire to use research as a tool for social change". (Duncan-Andrade & Morrell, 2008, p. 15). Because very few models exist for pursuing this type of work, we forged the path as we walked it, alongside our graduate students. Fortunately, the Chican@ students we worked with undertook their graduate studies because they were motivated by a desire to read, study, and produce knowledge that could lead to visible social changes, especially in Chican@ communities, and were willing to journey with us. Collectively, we negotiated (sometimes more successfully than others) the demands of academia with the material realities of the working-class community members with whom we worked, and our multiple roles as scholar activists in a traditional university space.

None of the 13 graduate research assistants we worked with over the years knew what to expect when first placed with the partnership. As the founders and directors of Adelante, we readily acknowledge that without them, the implementation of Adelante would never have been possible. As a result, when people ask, "How did you manage to develop so many programmatic components and sustain the partnership for so many years?", we always point to the Chican@ activist emerging scholars as essential to the day-to-day coordination, relationship and trust building, and creative and authentic research methods we were able to employ. The emerging scholars were immersed in a bustling, dynamic, and uncertain environment that required them to be self-motivated, effective communicators, quick learners and analytical thinkers who were able to bring their bodymindspirit into their graduate studies. In essence, they, too, were required to be nepantler@s as they balanced differing priorities, perspectives, and identities as social justice workers. For most, being nepantler@s came naturally. Socorro Morales worked with the partnership from 2011 to 2016. Reflecting on her experience and the engagement she and her peers had with Adelante, she describes the uniqueness of her research and career preparation:

> Working with Adelante provided a kind of graduate school training that was crucial to our professional careers. First, engaging with essentially a cohort of other graduate students is in and of itself a huge advantage. Right from the start, you enter a community of scholars where we each shared the ability to mentor others, and be mentored. Additionally, as students we had the rare opportunity to essentially meet with our professors/advisors (Dolores and Enrique) every week,

for 2 hours. Even though our discussions were often focused on the programmatic aspect of Adelante, I found it useful as a student to have constant access to my advisor, for both minor questions as well as program milestones, such as taking exams. Over the course of my years working with the partnership, I learned from observing and conversing with other students that we were able to develop a relationship with Dolores and Enrique, as well as with one another, that looked different from traditional models of graduate programs. In many ways, we found that as students, our practice was braided like a trenza with our theoretical perspectives, and our commitment to communities of color and Latin@ youth. Though I describe the partnership as one that I feel has helped me grow substantially as a scholar and person, I am by no means suggesting that it was easy or straightforward. In fact, for me the partnership work that I engaged in provided numerous growing pains and points of contention that I utilized to become the scholar I am today. It became disheartening at times to know some teachers were not going to change. It became frustrating when elementary school students who clearly brought familial knowledge with them into the classroom would still take up and perform colonial and deficit discourses. What I learned in working with Adelante was that the realities of activist scholarship are never simple. And I also learned that aside from that work being difficult, it was sometimes criticized and challenged by "armchair" revolutionaries in higher education who could argue about Foucault all day, but did not know how to talk with 1st-graders and translate theory into practice. I learned what it really means to effect the change that you so desire and write about in graduate school.

Socorro describes the constant state of nepantla the graduate students found themselves in, operating in a liminal space that fuses theory and practice, evoking both dissonance and transformation at Jackson Elementary. She and the other nepantler@s took the theories they were studying and were able to translate them into meaningful practices. Together with the Adelante graduate students, we all learned to be somewhat at home in nepantla, and to embrace the choques and dissonance. All of them have already begun to or will soon take their research training into the communities, schools, and universities where they work after completing graduate school. Being at home with the nepantla that is inherent in community-based, activist scholarship situated in Eurocentric and colonial educational institutions has been one of the most difficult and useful lessons we have learned.

TRANSAS: MANEUVERING, STRATEGIZING, AND POSITIONING ACROSS EDUCATIONAL INSTITUTIONS

El que no transa, no avanza. (S/he who does not conduct transactions does not advance.)

—Urrieta, 2009, p. 11

In his discussion of transas, Urrieta (2009) describes how Chican@ activist educators utilize their daily calculated practices or strategic moves to advance and benefit the marginalized students in their educational sites. His participants enacted their transas—sometimes planned and other times spontaneous—as a method for challenging their institutions and creating spaces for change. We similarly view the strategies we employed to coordinate, fund, grow, and sustain Adelante as transas. Arguing that transas must begin with centering the interests of students and communities of color, we employed strategies that enabled us to maneuver within the educational institutions and community spaces we had access to because of our roles as faculty members, parents, members of the local community, or experts in Chican@Latin@ education. Although we were sometimes forced to respond to the immediate situation at hand, the tactics we used in building and sustaining Adelante were usually deliberate and intentional. Below, we offer three examples of the calculated transas we pursued that made the Adelante Partnership possible: (1) growing and funding the partnership, (2) framing community partnership work as engaged scholarship, and (3) building relationships with allies and others.

Strategic Growth: Programs, Funding, and Team Members

Perhaps our wisest and most strategic transa took place in the spring of 2005 as we planned for the pilot year of Adelante. Deciding to start small, with 47 kindergartners in two classrooms, was a difficult decision to make because, in actuality, there were few differences between the kindergarten students we initially targeted and those students we did not include. We did not want to reinforce the type of dual-track programs that already operate in many schools; however, we had to consider our limited financial and human resources. Despite the critique we received from various teachers and leaders who felt that limiting access to field trips and mentors in the first year to dual-language kindergartners was unfair and discriminatory, we knew that striving for high-quality programming while also building toward authentic relationships with parents and families could not be accomplished if we overextended ourselves. This was a disconcerting and uncomfortable dilemma for us, but in hindsight, phasing in our partnership ensured our survival in year 1 and beyond.

In strategically managing growth, we were ultimately able to incorporate subsequent cohorts of students on an annual basis and to reach our goal of working with the whole school, kindergarten through 6th grade, dual-immersion and non-dual-immersion. By year 7, we had made inroads with Bryant Middle School, into which the majority of Jackson students fed, and with the Mestizo Arts and Activism (MAA) collective, a Westside Salt Lake high school group that would eventually serve some of the original cohort of Adelante students. Thus, resisting the notion that a whole-school approach in year 1 was the only way to commence the partnership provided us with the space and time we needed to get to know parents, work with fewer teachers initially, and begin aligning our goals with the broader community, including stakeholders at the university.

Moreover, our cumulative approach to growing the partnership enabled us to grow into our roles as fundraisers. Indeed, by the spring of 2013, the partnership team consisted of six full-time, fully funded graduate students assigned to four sites in the school district and at the university. Our collaboration with key offices, a few committed university administrators, and the school district resulted in the institutionalization of programs and a continuing investment in graduate student funding. We forged relationships with both academic and student affairs[1] units at the university and reached out to organizations that funded programming for underrepresented populations or first-generation students. The breadth and variety of university, social service, local foundation, and state agency organizations enabled us to leverage funding sources for the staffing, programmatic, and research goals that we had each year. Although we were never successful at getting one of our larger (more than $50,000) research grants funded, we became adept at constructing a patchwork system of funding graduate students and subsidizing the costs of university field trips, science camps, and all the other Adelante components.

The challenge of not only maintaining but also growing the partnership every year required us to employ creative funding transas. We leveraged across our two academic departments, several other university units, and various research grants to successfully fund graduate students—by far our biggest annual expenditure. For example, we negotiated with department heads to fund one graduate student for each student we could fund with external funding. Thus, it was critical that when we won several smaller grants from local foundations or multiple $50,000 grants from the Utah System of Higher Education, we covered graduate students and not just programmatic line items such as transportation, T-shirts for students, or science camp expenses, so that we could leverage the university funding necessary for additional graduate students. We understand these different phased, community-building, and institutionalizing transas as necessary for expanding and sustaining the partnership. These transas were centered both on the need to fund programs for youth and their families and to fund graduate research assistantships for the Chican@ graduate students on the partnership team.

Communicating, Framing, and Emphasizing Adelante's Purpose

When scholars engage or conduct activist scholarship with communities of color, the work is very often framed as service or outreach. Though we were clearly scholarly in our activist approach, our research, especially in the early years, was consistently portrayed and devalued as community service or program development by many university faculty and administrators. Many viewed the sight of elementary students with red Adelante T-shirts on campus favorably. However, it was also more often than not characterized as outreach fit for full-time staff, not full-time scholars. Thus, it was essential for us to consistently talk about the research we conducted, about the changes to school culture we experienced, and the impact to college students' expectations and aspirations that we documented.

Again, we framed Adelante as a community-engaged scholarship model, not a community outreach program. Professionally, as mid- and early-career scholars, we never lost sight of the retention, promotion, and tenure (RPT) policies at our research-intensive institution. The standards by which we would be evaluated and judged were clear in our minds and undoubtedly informed our decisions both to grow strategically and to present and publish our scholarly contributions in peer-reviewed outlets. We used the language of the university as a transa, describing our research topics in the academic language of engaged scholarship, critical service learning, first-year experiences for undergraduates, and first-generation retention rates. We made sure that our vitas, and those of our graduate students, characterized the relationship building, program coordination, and event planning as community-engaged research activities and not outreach. Indeed, these activities were necessary for the day-to-day operation of the partnership, but they also enabled us to connect with community leaders, build confianza, understand the material realities of living and surviving in this community, and document the aspirations of the Chican@Latin@ elementary students and university students of color who participated in our programming.

While we took care to frame our scholarship to our colleagues and the larger academic community, we simultaneously worked to communicate with our network of partners across institutions and organizations that might be willing to share resources and sustain programs. Beginning in September 2008, Adelante published a monthly partnership newsletter that Jackson Elementary students in grades K–3 took home to their parents and that was emailed electronically to community partners.[2] Initially distributed to this small audience, the newsletter soon evolved to not only inform the entire school community of partnership events, but also to provide a platform for keeping both university and community allies informed of and invested in the partnership. For example, the content notified parents about free vaccinations being held in the school cafeteria or highlighted the innovative practices of Jackson's "Teacher of the Month." Simultaneously, university partners could read about undergraduate students volunteering during the school's annual Halloween carnival or university faculty hosting Jackson students in their science lab or engineering classroom. Our aim was clear: We sought to reinforce the messages of college awareness and expectations while also announcing upcoming activities and keeping all of Adelante's stakeholders informed of the many positive things going on at Jackson.

The April 2011 newsletter, in particular, is a noteworthy example of how we purposefully framed our scholarship, emphasized the partnership's goals, and stressed community knowledge. This newsletter announced that Adelante won the American Educational Research Association (AERA) Paulo Freire Award for Social Justice scholarship and described how Adelante's graduate students presented research regarding their partnership work at the annual National Association of Chicana/Chicano Studies (NACCS) conference in Pasadena, California. In addition, it showcased the Oral History Project's digital assignments completed by 5th-graders and how Jackson students visited the federal courthouse and practiced public-speaking activities at a law school camp. The calculated strategy to compile and narrate the multiple levels of engagement, leadership, and research, across a wide array of partners, exemplifies a transa intended to secure the sustainability of the partnership.

Partnership Building Is Relationship Building

Though starting small, growing strategically, and framing our work were essential functions to the partnership's development and its sustainability, forging relationships was perhaps the most important function of our work. Our transas and our outcomes differed greatly depending on whether we were developing relationships with allies and those who we worked on be-half of or with those who held deficit views about the Jackson community and did not share Adelante's social justice agenda. Our transas for build-ing relationships with the former were much more successful than with the latter.

For example, our team of graduate students was deliberately recruited and selected. Funding and working with young, committed, and aspiring critical scholars was an intentional transa that enabled us to cultivate the requisite relationships with students and families at Jackson. Graduate stu-dents, as the faces of Adelante, played an essential role, often as the first con-tact with students and family members. Their bilingualism, biculturalism, and ability to connect with and be dedicated to this community garnered trust and quickly situated all of us as legitimate partners with parent leaders and community advocates. In Chapter 4, we discussed in detail about the confianza that was developed with parents. That confianza was particularly evident twice when the future of Adelante was threatened and parents re-sponded with support in a very public way. As shared in the Introduction, after the first year when a school leader stated that she was terminating the partnership, parents met over the summer to respond and be ready to advocate on behalf of their children. In 2014, when parents learned that the university might negatively impact Adelante's future existence, more than 100 Jackson parents sent letters and signatures to the university president, communicating their displeasure regarding the decisions being made with-out community involvement. Clearly, the deep relationships the graduate students and we built with Adelante parents and students were crucial to building and sustaining the partnership.

However, it was relationships with those who held deficit views or were unsupportive of the partnership work that were most challenging. Indeed, our transa was sometimes avoidance or minimal contact with these indi-viduals, and this, of course, was not the most effective strategy. At the time, we did not consider Anzaldúa's nos/otras as a transa or even a way to under-stand the importance of building relationships with teachers who held deficit views. By partially dividing nos/otras into two, Anzaldúa affirms our need to work collectively, yet also acknowledges the divisiveness that was so often felt in the relationships with some teachers. In hindsight, nos/otras and the following example illustrate how missed opportunities prevented us from forging stronger unity with many teachers. Below, Neri Oliva, a graduate student who was the parent engagement coordinator, tells us about a parent concern that was communicated to her after cofacilitating one of the parent engagement meetings:

A parent who attended the meeting was expressing her concerns about Ms. Janero. She said that Janero always closes the door on students [in the morning, as soon as the bell rings] even if they are a few steps away and her daughter is really scared to be late. The mother said that she closes the door on all the Latin@ kids and "que eso es racismo." She also spoke about another time when she was scheduled to meet with Janero and Janero told her to leave because the mother didn't show up with a translator. The mother told her that her daughter's dad was on his way and he could translate and Janero said no. So what do we do about things like this? This isn't the first time a parent talks about Janero. Is there someone parents can talk to at the district level since the Jackson administrators know what's going on [and nothing has been done about this]?

Consistently, we were confronted with scenarios like this one and were prompted to self-reflectively ask: How do we build bridges with those who do not agree with Adelante's core principles or do not recognize the assets in the Jackson students and families? In this case, we communicated with administrative staff and worked with Neri to engage the mother in advocacy for her child, but we failed at working with the teacher directly. We strategically chose to avoid the teacher and focused on helping the parent maneuver around the teacher in order to advocate for her child.

Our transa was not, however, always avoidance. We did try our best to build bridges with teachers, educational leaders, administrators, and even some parents who did not agree with the partnership's core goals, activities, or strategies. This meant always pushing for more frequent and effective forms of communication, especially with teachers, and for new ways to bring them into the planning and decisionmaking without overburdening them. Yet, given our limited time and resources, we very often went the easier route by focusing on the many positive relationships with parents, undergraduate and graduate students, and those teachers who did not need to be convinced that students as young as 5 years old should be made aware of higher educational opportunities and be expected to reach for and achieve whatever goals they set.

Although it was a struggle to develop and maintain relationships with people like Ms. Janero, sustainability of partnerships is partially dependent on people like her. Anzaldúa's theoretical idea of nos/otras has helped us theorize the work that needs to be done when people who occupy vastly different cultural realities need to work together. That is, nos/otras offers a unique way to acknowledge the divisiveness that has sometimes been expressed or

felt between teachers/leaders/administrators and the Adelante team. In looking back, we see that we needed to do more to bridge the divide and help
join the nos and otras together to bridge the relationships with "others." If
transas must begin with centering the interests of students and communities
of color, then in order to create transformative ruptures, we must find ways
to work with those who do not share the same social justice agenda. It is
these transformative ruptures that we turn to in the next section.

TRANSFORMATIVE RUPTURES:
A PATHWAY TO CHICAN@ EDUCATION

Scholars, activists, and educators interested in initiating an Adelante-type
partnership often ask us how we measure success given that L@s Primer@s
are not yet old enough to enroll in college. Although we plan to follow
up with them one more time at the end of their senior year to assess their
college-going plans, we have shifted away from college-going rates and standardized test scores as the primary or sole metrics for measuring Adelante's
success. We question and critique the need for high-stakes testing, yet until
there is a change to standardized testing, we welcome increased test scores
for Adelante students. We also want to see rising GPAs, increased enrollment in college-preparatory courses, and eventual college attendance and
degree attainment. However, we know that these standard measures of academic outcomes are difficult to achieve because of the indestructibility of
racism and the pervasiveness of intersecting oppressions in the everyday
lives of Adelante students and their families. Barriers brought about by an
unforgiving economy, dehumanizing immigration policies, and a disadvan-
tageous public school system have impacted the lives of Adelante students
and their families and challenged the partnership's ability to create seamless
direct pathways to higher education.

It was not until we broadened our understandings of success and change
that we were able to understand transformative ruptures as a powerful tool
for recognizing the momentary or micro-level, but very significant, changes
that we were observing within the partnership. Transformative ruptures enable us to see how individuals, families, and the partnership collective can
enact incidents, interactions, experiences, and moments that challenge inequity, racism, colonialism, and oppression. We have not ceased to see racial
realism or pervasive coloniality in this community, the school, or the university, but we have been able to maintain a critical hope (Duncan-Andrade,
2009) and a sense that triumph (Bell, 1992) can be achieved in moments
where transformative ruptures can be cultivated, promoted, and replicated.

Though transformative ruptures come in countless forms, here we discuss three types that were common to our work and are indicators of success. First, we note the disruptions to educational structures that push against the normative practices, policies, cultures, or spaces in K–16 schooling. We then discuss transformative ruptures to colonial methodologies that challenge what counts as research and emphasize bringing one's bodymindspirit to the research process. Finally, we look at how disruptions to everyday reality can allow educators, scholars, students, and community members to envision and imagine a very different future.

Transforming Physical Space

The physical transformation of the school and the allocation of space at Jackson in the past 10 years has also been a transformative rupture. As we described in Chapter 1, the school went from ordinary, plain white walls that some described as mimicking a detention facility to a vibrant space with painted hallways in shades of purple, red, green, and orange. Along with new paint to demarcate the different grade levels, teachers were encouraged to show pride in their favorite college and hang logos and pennants of their alma mater to further promote college expectation. The current principal instituted a college T-shirt Friday where teachers and students can sport shirts from their favorite schools. Inspirational quotes by notable leaders such as Sitting Bull, Malala Yousafzai, Nelson Mandela, and Gandhi, in both English and Spanish, are now visible throughout the school. One quote by Malcolm X, painted above a bulletin board in the main hallway, states: "Education is our passport to the future, for tomorrow belongs to the people who prepare for today."

In addition to visible physical changes, the occupation of space within the school by the Adelante team has made a real impact to the culture and energy of Jackson. In the first couple of years, the partnership did not have any designated space for holding planning and organizational meetings. As always, space is a premium commodity in schools, so when one of the principals offered us an unused storage space located down an empty hallway, behind the faculty lounge and past the copy room, we were more than happy to accept the offer. Two of our graduate students were able to have regular office hours, and parents began to drop by for a plática or to ask a question about an upcoming event. Later, Adelante shared a more centrally located classroom with teachers and staff who on some days needed it for testing, parent meetings, and individualized instruction. Although sharing was inconvenient at times, our presence in a core classroom made the partnership visible to students and parents on a daily basis and provided a space for weekly meetings. By 2012, our final meeting place became a classroom located at the center of the school. It quickly emerged into what has become a very active parent–community room with college pennants, new organizing shelves for storage of ballet folklórico costumes, and an often-used coffee maker, refrigerator, and worktables sized for children and adults. The partnership's presence and the presence of Brown bodies, including parent leaders, Chican@ graduate students, and a steady stream of undergraduate students of color has contributed to a visual and ideological transformative rupture that validates the presence and knowledge of Brown bodies and counters deep-seated and deficit ideologies about students of color.

Disrupting Colonial Methodologies

We believe that the critical race feminista praxis we have been involved with for more than 10 years provides examples of a different kind of transformative rupture, one that chips away at the White supremacist and colonial logic that often establishes what counts as "good" research. For too long, this majoritarian worldview has meant that researchers have conducted their research in ways that exploit marginalized communities as research sites and students and people of color as research "subjects," taking from them without giving anything back (Denzin & Lincoln, 2003). For too long, it has translated into researchers who attempt to approach their research in disengaged ways as unbiased and supposedly neutral beings. As we mentioned above in our discussion of graduate student training, our research, from the start, has been very different, as it is grounded in a goal of collaboration, advocacy, social change, and reciprocity.

Though we have fallen short in our ideal goals of sharing our research with Adelante participants and co-collaborating in the research process, there were meaningful ways in which we did both. For example, we moved beyond only sharing our research findings in traditional academic journals and have shared our research with parents (via bilingual community presentations), teachers and principals (via professional development, dialogue, and distribution of publications), and mentors (via group pláticas) in the hopes of creating opportunities for transformation with various participants. As we discussed in Chapter 5, we also presented research to our campus colleagues, including administrators, faculty, staff, and students, to build key relationships across campus and to help them view Adelante as core part of the university's community engagement goals. These campus presentations often created transformative ruptures where university folks had to rethink the university's role as a reciprocal partner with local schools and historically marginalized communities.

At times, the collaboration has moved beyond just sharing to really engaging in co-creating and co-presenting research. Collectively, we and/ or our graduate students have presented at national conferences with class-room teachers, Spanish-speaking mothers, and elementary school students. In fact, one of our proudest transformative moments was watching 5th-graders present their work that emerged from their after-school Chican@ studies class with Sylvia Mendoza and Socorro Morales at the National As-sociation for Chicana and Chicano Studies conference in the spring of 2014. Witnessing 11 sharply dressed 5th-graders, sitting at the front of a hotel conference room, facing a standing-room-only audience, was transforma-tive in numerous ways. First, based on the smiling faces, sighs of relief, and debriefing conversations that the students had with Sylvia and Socorro after the presentation, it was a transformative experience for both students and their families. Students were able to be the experts and authors of their own experiences. Similarly, it was also a clear disruption to the traditional ways in which academia considers who is a knower, a producer of knowledge, and a researcher.

Our critical race feminista praxis has also been a transformative rup- ture to the idea that research is strictly a cerebral or academic task. We have brought our bodymindspirit to the research process in ways that we never fully anticipated. When the media, educational studies, or educators maintain low expectations for Latin@ children or refer to Latin@ parents and commu-nity members as lacking, uninvolved, unsupportive, or not future oriented, it is our Brown bodies and the bodies of our birth children that provide the living connection between the deficit discourses and educational practices. When college students of color are struggling to keep a roof over their head or to find professional support for their mental illness, it hurts our spirit, and we must act swiftly. Indeed, acknowledging and validating the tremendous efforts, and sometimes heroic ways, in which the Jackson students, their fami-lies, and their college mentors have survived, thrived, and persevered despite systems of inequity has often meant a realignment of the research process.

For example, themes related to citizenship and immigration were the focus of our first article (Delgado Bernal et al., 2008), but were not at the forefront of our original research plan, which highlighted college awareness and expectations. However, as the national debate on immigration and un-documented people turned more xenophobic, Adelante facilitated spaces where students and their family members could start to voice their despair, protest proposed legislation, or find needed legal services. It was obvious that parents cared about their children's education and wanted the oppor-tunities for them to attend and succeed in college, but what emerged more than anything was fear and concern for their bodies, the welfare of their families, and the future of their place in U.S. society. Tending to the needs of this community, fostering discussions, and noting some participants' vulnerability required a disruption to our own understandings of the research and publishing process as well as a willingness to bring our heart, intellect, and bodies to the process.

Ruptures to What Can Be Imagined

Pues ahora se que ellos pueden seguir estudiando. Pueden seguir superando. Y antes nos habían dicho que no, verdad, que nada mas hasta, se puede decir la prepa. Que ellos no podían seguir aquí a la universidad. Pero, ahora se que pues si hay modo de que ellos puedan seguir adelante. (Well, now I know that, they [our children] can continue studying. They can continue bettering themselves. Before they [society] had told us no, that they could only study up to high school and that they couldn't attend the university here. But now I know that there is a way that they can continue moving forward.)

—Immigrant mother of a Jackson student

College is not only a possibility for them [kindergartners], but it is something they can achieve. And it's something that's not just a possibility, but it's also something we are going to talk about on a regular basis.

—Jackson kindergarten teacher

I'm going to be roommates with Berta when we come to the U and I'm going to have a purple bedspread and lots of pillows.

—Joslin, Jackson 3rd-grade student

Each of the above quotes, by a mother, a teacher, and a 3rd-grader, help illustrate what Anzaldúa (1987) means when she says, "Nothing happens in the 'real' world unless it first happens in the images in our heads" (p. 87). Through these quotes, one can understand transformative ruptures as chipping away at structures of oppression that allow us to dream audaciously and work toward something different. Some may say that transformative ruptures emphasize an incrementalist approach, especially when they take place at the individual level. However, we believe there is hope and possibility when young people talk about "when" they go to college, when immigrant parents want their child in a Spanish dual-immersion program because it will help him or her in college, or when teachers engage in conversations that question their own biases. Though the quotes above do not reflect college-going rates nor test scores, we find success in their words; they exemplify a transformative rupture to what can be imagined and believed.

Disruptions to everyday reality can allow educators, scholars, students, and community members to envision and imagine a very different future. For example, the regular field trips that were organized and coordinated with the medical school, the law school, or modern dance department disrupted the everyday reality of young Jackson students (and their parents), allowing them, even if momentarily, to picture themselves as medical professionals, lawyers, or professional dancers. The frequent weekly conversations with college students of color throughout their elementary school years became Jackson students' reality, which allowed them to dream about when they are in college. We believe that the cultural affirmation that was nurtured through the Oral History Project inspired them to be proud of who they are and recognize the resiliency in their own families. It is difficult to calculate the exact impact of these different encounters on the aspirations of young people, but in Chapter 3 many of the data from L@s Primer@s point to how their engagement in these activities have indeed shaped their future aspirations. After 10 years of programming and relationship building, images of going to college, being leaders in their own community, and pursuing a career that makes them "happy" have filled the heads not only of Jackson students, but of many of their parents and a number of their teachers.

Anzaldúa's idea pushes us to link the micro and macro—what happens in our heads with what happens in the world around us. We understand her to be asking us to imagine equitable structures, just institutions, and fair schooling practices in the face of indestructible and intersecting oppressions. Many activist educators have done just that—reimagined educational institutions as they work with various marginalized communities of color to create spaces, moments, and opportunities for transformative ruptures to occur individually, structurally, and collectively (Cammarota & Romero, 2014; Duncan-Andrade & Morrell, 2008; Kohli & Pizarro, 2016; Stovall, 2016; Tintiangco-Cubales, Daus-Magbual, & Daus-Magbual, 2010; Urrieta, 2009; Valenzuela, 2016). We also believe that university and college administrators and faculty members should seek to reimagine how their institutions can do more to foster community-based partnerships and to develop K–16 educational pathways initiatives. The underlying mission of most public universities is to serve the community in which they are located. Taking tangible steps and implementing specific strategies that promote collaboration, enrichment, and engaged learning for underrepresented students should be part of this reimagining.

On a personal level, our ability to reimagine educational institutions, systems, and policies is partially what has allowed us to keep doing this work for over a decade. It has also allowed us to understand success in multiple ways. So, although we continue to believe that the "outcome of partnership work or community engaged scholarship is but a brief disruption, a moment in a legacy of oppressive structures imbedded in schools and society" (Alemán, Delgado Bernal, & Mendoza, 2013, p. 335), we also simultaneously understand the outcomes to be transformative ruptures to oppressive structures that can allow us to hold images in our head that breed hope and coalitional resistance.

CONCLUSION

As co-founders and co-directors of Adelante, we discovered the obvious: that creating and implementing the partnership did not occur in a linear fashion and could not evolve without moments of frustration, failure, risk, self-reflection, or refinement of our tactics and programs. Sustainability required a broad approach—a critical race feminista praxis—that allowed us to bring our bodymindspirit to our work and merge social activism with a spiritual vision of transforming inequities. This praxis affirms Brown bodies, challenges how they are "othered" and regulated in schools and society, has shaped our programming (for example, the Oral History Project, mentors of color, ballet folklórico, and Padres en Acción/Parents in Action), and has influenced our approaches to research (data collection that relied heavily on the experiential knowledge of students and families of color as well as relationships of confianza). Put differently, our development of Adelante was strategic, and both its infrastructure and our methodology were grounded in the principles of CRTs and Chicana feminist theories.

A critical race feminista praxis, by definition, requires a multitude of transas. Our transas allowed us to partner with decisionmakers, often by framing the significance of the partnership's goals with the missions of K–12 and higher educational institutions, local foundations, and community organizations. Although these transas made sustaining programmatic elements more feasible, we wrestled with which tactics to use, striving never to lose sight of our ultimate goals and primary stakeholders—the Chican@Latin@ youth, students of color, and the families in this community. As scholar activists, our transas also meant drawing upon the relations of power associated with our different roles in different contexts as parents, professors, researchers, and community members. Various transas aided us in developing and sustaining programs and initiatives, while also allowing us to navigate and subvert the historically disadvantaging educational processes that are embedded within the institutions in which we work. Though our transas continue to be works in progress, we understand that transforming educational pathways for Chican@Latin@ students requires us to develop and sustain programs that specifically incite transformative ruptures. Via a critical race feminista praxis, spaces, moments, and incidents of transformative rupture can be cultivated, challenging the racism and colonial logic that shape unjust practices, structures, and policies.

We came to learn that blending our political and strategic transas with the tension and conflict inherent in the relationship-building aspect of partnership work was at times risky, but the resulting choques often created the conditions for transformative ruptures to occur. Having a macro-level perspective of the history of unequal education and an understanding of the pervasive racism of educational policies and practices across educational institutions (Alemán, 2007; Alemán & Alemán, 2010; Delgado Bernal, 1999; Delgado Bernal & Villalpando, 2002), we eventually embraced and began to leverage the choques in mindsets, ideologies, and perspectives as a method for destabilizing racist structures and decentering the majoritarian stories that influenced and drove educational practice at Jackson. Moreover, having a micro-level perspective of the importance of affirming cultural knowledges, languages, histories, and stories, Adelante refused to let Jackson students and their families' talent, energy, knowledge, resilience, and activism go unacknowledged or be devalued. Our critical race feminista praxis remains grounded in an enduring commitment to center and affirm the stories, identities, and histories of Chican@Latin@ students via various transas and amid frequent choques in order to provoke transformative ruptures. Indeed, what we personally found most rewarding and inspiring was spending our time and efforts centering students and their family members as "holders and creators of knowledge" (Delgado Bernal, 2002) or interacting and working with them as active leaders in the community. In addition, preparing graduate students to engage their research agendas as scholar activists and institutionalizing university spaces for undergraduate mentors to succeed and thrive emerged as key aspects of our pathways approach. Although these relationships and endeavors often demanded our time and caused us to neglect other key aspects of the partnership, the students, activists, leaders, and partners nurtured our souls and taught us what it means to struggle for educational equity.

We now understand and can articulate a critical race feminista praxis as an indispensable and malleable framework for conducting social justice research and partnership building. With CRTs and Chicana feminist epistemologies guiding and challenging us, critical race feminista praxis is a way that we do our work, a rationale for doing it, and a way forward as we seek to create more opportunities for disrupting systemic oppression. What we have attempted to do in this chapter, and really throughout the book, is to provide examples of what critical race feminista praxis looks like, rather than a prescription that says, "This is the model for doing partnership work." We look forward to engaging in future examples of critical race feminista praxis while also continuing to learn from the praxis of others who are transforming educational pathways for Chican@Latin@ students.

Epilogue

We include this brief epilogue in order to provide an update on the Adelante partnership and on our personal involvement beyond the decade we write about. Our commitment to the partnership has been a long-term one that continues to this day. However, personal circumstances have changed and our professional careers have shifted in different directions. As a result, we no longer live in the local community and our day-to-day involvement with and leadership of Adelante looks very different from how it did during the first decade of its development.

I (Enrique) went back home to Texas, where at least four previous generations of my family have lived and worked their whole lives. As a faculty member and chair of Educational Leadership and Policy Studies at the University of Texas at San Antonio, I am currently working to initiate and implement similar partnerships in South Texas. I continue to consult with Dolores, and with the current Jackson principal, about how to continue the Adelante programs we initiated, and I am always inspired by the updates on the amazing initiatives and partnerships that have been sustained. For example, in June 2016, Jackson was highlighted on the local news when former students, who were graduating from high school, participated in the first-ever graduation walk through the halls of Jackson.[1] Marching in their cap and gown, these students showed the elementary students a milestone they can strive for on their educational journey. One of those graduates, a former Jackson student, was highlighted as she walked the halls and hugged some of her younger siblings. Her mother, who served as the Adelante parent liaison for 3 years, continues to shape parent leadership and to work with the faculty and administration in positive and innovative ways. My last two graduate students at the University of Utah are in the process of completing their dissertation studies with Adelante participants; this is something I am proud of. Although it was difficult to leave this community and the friendships that were formed in the 11 years I worked with Adelante stakeholders, students, and families in Utah, the opportunity to go home and to apply the knowledge and expertise that I have developed in my early career to the problems and challenges faced in my community in South Texas, was something Sonya and I could not pass up.

I (Dolores) need to name the angst I feel around my departure and sub-sequent return to Adelante. My family and I moved away from Utah in the spring of 2014 without saying good-bye to Adelante families and teachers or local community workers, without saying where I was going, without saying if I would be back. This type of departure did not align with the Chicana feminista ideas that have guided me for over 20 years, or with the impor-tance placed on the relational aspects of the work I had collectively done with Enrique and all the members of the Adelante team. Mostly because I was in my own personal and professional nepantla—a place of extreme pain, confusion, chaos, and transition—I felt I could not say good-bye. I had to protect myself and my family, and in doing so, I felt I could not be open and honest with a community that I had lived within and grown to love dur-ing the previous 10 years. When I came back to my faculty position at the University of Utah (but not to live in Utah) in the fall of 2015, my position as the Adelante director transitioned into something very different. My role is less hands-on and more advisory, budgetary, advocacy, and supportive of those administering the different partnership components. The transition has been difficult, but it is one that has continued to lend itself to the institu-tionalization of Adelante.

In fact, institutionalization has been a goal since the first year of the partnership. We remember often saying to each other that we did not want the partnership to be solely dependent upon us for sustainability. We would say, "If you're gone or if I'm gone, or we're both gone, Adelante should still continue." Our goal was to not only find ways to sustain and grow the partnership, but to institutionalize it and strengthen the relationships among community, district, and university partners in a way that would ensure the partnership's success into the future. Today, Adelante is sustained and continues to serve the Jackson community because of the committed school leadership and numerous aspects of the partnership that have been insti-tutionalized within the school, district, and university. One example that best exemplifies this is the district's commitment to fund a position that can carry on Adelante activities. The district hired Alicia De Leon, a university doctoral candidate, with hardline funding as a Community Learning Cen-ter coordinator. Among other responsibilities, she serves as the university liaison and coordinator for Adelante activities, including field trips and par-ent engagement. Another example of sustainability is evident in the cur-rent principal's hiring of Cinthia Cervantes-Castañeda, a former graduate student who worked with Adelante. Cinthia worked for two years as a full-time classroom teacher who held high expectations, engaged her students in cultural affirmation, and demonstrated a commitment to Jackson families, while also serving as the after-school ballet folklórico director/teacher. She recently (fall 2016) moved to another Title I school within the district and will certainly share her skills and talents with the students and families there. Liliana Castrellon continues to coordinate the undergraduate mentors as a full-time doctoral student for the Ethnic Studies Program at the university. As we explained in Chapter 5, the mentoring component has become somewhat institutionalized, and her position is paid for by the university, not Adelante grant funding.

We understand that Adelante and Jackson continue to evolve, especially during the past few years, and we are confident that our transitions have left the partnership in a strong position, both financially and programmatically. Jackson has a committed and strong educational leader, Dr. Jana Edward. At the beginning of her tenure, the school was named by the district as a Community Learning Center, a designation that will no doubt assist the leadership and faculty in aligning the goals and activities of Adelante further into the fabric of the school. Under her direction and with the leadership of former vice principal Lamar Spotted Elk, Jackson became one of two schools in Utah and 114 low-income schools across the country to implement a significant initiative as part of an Apple ConnectEd grant. Rolled out in April 2016, this initiative includes school preparation and teacher training; iPads, Apple TVs, and Mac computers for teachers; iPads for every student; and instructional coaching and technical support for teachers for 3 years after implementation. Much of the way the grant was written included the partnership model and frameworks that Adelante helped facilitate with Dr. Edward and Mr. Spotted Elk. As we transitioned out of our full-time partnership co-director responsibilities, we also left behind a university grant that was capable of funding university visits, graduate students, and parental engagement activities for an additional 2 years.

Hardline funding and these kinds of highly visible Apple grant or university funds lend themselves to long-term sustainability and the institutionalization of partnerships. However, even more important are the leaders, allies, and stakeholders who are committed to the partnership's goals and are willing to do the work needed to dismantle deficit thinking, ensure educational excellence for all students, and nurture cultural/racial affirmation. Along with our own transitions, there have been transitions in the superintendent's office at the Salt Lake City School District and the Dean's Office in the College of Education at the university. New leadership in the Office of the Vice President for Equity and Diversity is currently reviewing the sustainability of the mentoring component of the partnership via the Diversity Scholars Program. As is often the case in higher education and other educational organizations, new leadership sometimes decides to change course and to implement their own initiatives.

What we can say today, however, is that Adelante and Jackson continue to provide college awareness and expectation programs for all the students within the school's walls. Parents continue to lead in a number of capacities, and teachers continue to work with staff to plan field trips and utilize the talents and energy of undergraduate mentors. Ballet folklórico has been sustained as an after-school program, and there are plans to reinitiate the Oral History Program, which was not implemented during the 2015–2016 academic year. The partnership has indeed been sustained beyond any one or two individuals. Our vision of distributing leadership opportunities and of stimulating a college-going culture across the school and community has been realized. Our hope is that Adelante will continue to serve as a tool for transforming educational pathways for Chican@Latin@ students and for all students at Jackson.

Notes

Introduction

1. We use a nonitalicized format of Spanish words and only translate words to English if we deem it necessary at first use. Following Gloria Anzaldúa's example in her later work, we will use words in Spanish alongside the English without translation. The nonitalicized format and the use of Spanish without constant translation is our political and theoretical attempt to avoid "othering" the Spanish language and to require the monolingual English speaker to put forth additional effort to engage the ways of knowing in this book.

2. Our use of @ at the end of labels such as *Latin@* and *Chican@* is a way to recognize gender fluidity and to challenge the gender hierarchy and binary present in the Spanish language (the use of the masculine *o* at the end of words to refer to both males and females). When referring to males only, we use *Chicanos*, and if referring to females only we use *Chicanas*.

3. Dr. Octavio Villalpando was a cofounder of the Adelante partnership and subsequently ceased his directing responsibilities with the partnership after being named the University of Utah's associate vice president for equity and diversity in the spring of 2007.

4. *Chicana* and *Chicano* are cultural and political identities that were popularized during the Chicano Movement of the 1960s. They are composed of multiple layers and are identities of resistance that are often consciously adopted later in life. Though they most often refer to someone of Mexican origin, not all Mexican origin people embrace these terms, and there are non-Mexican origin Latin@s who do. We use these terms to refer to ourselves or broadly to a field of study (Chican@ education and Chican@ studies). We pair the political and cultural meaning of Chican@ with Latin@ and use *Chican@Latin@* to be inclusive of all ethnic groups included in the umbrella term *Latin@*, such as Guatemalans, Peruvians, and Chileans. We understand that collectively and individually our participants use many different terms to self-identify, and we use the term they use when they have noted it.

5. We intentionally use *anticolonial* instead of *decolonial/decolonized* in agreement with scholars such as Tuck and Yang (2012) and Calderón (2014), who argue that the latter concept has been stripped of its deeply political and territorial meanings relating to the repatriation of Indigenous land and life; it should not be a metaphor for other things we want to do to improve our societies and schools.

6. In this book, we draw from critical race theory and Latin@ critical race theory and refer to them collectively as critical race theories (CRTs).

7. For some examples of putting critical race theory into educational practice, see Cammarota and Romero (2011); Stovall, Lynn, Danley, and Martin (2009); and Stovall (2016). For some examples of Chicana feminist theory engaged with K–12 youth, see Cruz (2013); Jiménez (2014); Fránquiz, Avila, and Lewis (2013); Mendoza (2015); and Morales (2016).

Chapter 1

1. We do not use pseudonyms for the name of the school, school district, or university because our partnership work has been very public, with much print, broadcast, and electronic media coverage as well as presentations to the district, Utah System of Higher Education, and University of Utah. We use pseudonyms throughout the book for the names of elementary students, undergraduate mentors, parents, educators, and administrators. To ensure anonymity, we have also eliminated or altered identifying characteristics of individuals. However, in the final chapter, with permission, we use the names of three individuals who currently carry out the vision of Adelante.

2. *Brown* is most often used interchangeably with Chican@Latin@. However, sometimes, especially when talking about the presence of college students at Jackson Elementary School, it is used more generally to refer to students of color and the presence of non–European American bodies.

3. University Neighborhood Partners (UNP), the University of Utah's unit responsible for promoting and facilitating community-engaged research and partnerships, sponsored the call for proposals. The grant provided startup funds for 2 years: $5,000 in year 1 and $5,000 in year 2. Since this initial grant, UNP has served as an integral partner and provided numerous opportunities for us to continue our work.

4. More than 30 additional graduate students have volunteered in different capacities, and many of these as well as other students have been hired as Adelante summer science camp teachers. In addition, one undergraduate student, Victoria (Tory) Morales, worked with us for multiple years, and literally hundreds of undergraduate students have volunteered or completed service learning with Adelante.

5. With permission, we use the real names of our graduate assistants throughout the book to ensure that their work and commitments are acknowledged.

6. A judge's split ruling in 2014 scrapped key provisions of the controversial HB 497, including the "reasonable suspicion" language that would have allowed law officers to second-guess a person's immigration status based on stereotypes of race, ethnicity, or accent. Under the ruling, police are not allowed to stop or detain an individual just to verify immigration status, and the provision of the law that would have made it a state crime to harbor a person in the country illegally was eliminated.

7. See U.S. Census reports issued 2015 and 2016 in references.

8. See https://www.youtube.com/watch?v=kTrFSBtPKwk for an example of University of Utah tailgating produced by social commentators and entertainers, the 1491s.

Chapter 3

1. As mentioned in Chapter 1, it has been extremely difficult to follow this group of students as a result of attrition. There are many reasons for the attrition, including the fact that a few families received official letters asking them to leave because they did not live within school boundaries. These families were active in Adelante, and their children were primarily in the dual-immersion program. This is curious as, 2 years later, there was an effort to downsize the dual-immersion program, and part of the justification was that there was not enough interest and enrollment had declined.

2. Although we write very little about Ballet Folklórico de Adelante, the after-school Mexican folklore performance troupe, it has been an essential space for cultural affirmation and parental engagement since the first year of Adelante. Throughout the years, the dance group has grown under the direction of different teachers, including three who were university students: Tory Morales, Cinthia Cervantes-Castañeda, and Mónica Gonzalez. The group has been as large as 40 students and has performed for numerous city and community events such as those at the University of Utah, state capitol, Salt Lake City Library, Living Traditions Festival, and Hispanic Chamber of Commerce.

3. Established in 1980, AVID, Advancement Via Individual Determination, is a global nonprofit organization dedicated to closing the achievement gap by preparing all students for college and other postsecondary opportunities. See AVID.org for more information.

4. Chapter 5 focuses on the mentoring component of Adelante, which has included nearly 700 mentors and 15,000 service hours in the past decade. Coordinating so many mentors is a huge task that has been taken up by different graduate research assistants who work with ethnic studies faculty teaching these courses to provide high-quality service learning mentoring experiences. In particular, Judi Pérez-Torres and Liliana Castrellon have been instrumental in coordinating the service learning mentor experience and both have focused some of their research on mentoring and/or critical service learning.

5. In response to a 2nd-grade teacher's inquiry about wanting to bring more parents into her classroom as she did literacy work, graduate student Judith Flores Carmona initiated the Oral History Project in 2007 by starting with one lesson, "The Story of My Name," and then a photography project based on family stories. Under the direction of Sylvia Mendoza and Socorro Morales, the program grew over the years to include numerous digital projects, such as the "Music of My Home," and it was also expanded to an after-school Chican@ Studies class. For more information about the Oral History Project or the ethnic studies class, see Flores Carmona and Delgado Bernal (2012); Morales, Mendoza, and Delgado Bernal (2016); and Mendoza (2016).

6. Early in the partnership, the classrooms we worked with received four field trips per year, plus a weeklong science camp. As the partnership has grown, that has changed. All classrooms now have one field trip, with kindergarten and 6th grade re-

ceiving two per year as a way to begin and end their elementary school experience. The campus visits and activities have been implemented with support from an array of campus partners who provide hands-on activities or lessons in their particular department/unit. Throughout the years, numerous graduate students have served as a liaison between the campus partners and the Jackson teachers to align the field trip activities with the core curriculum.

7. For more information on the University of Utah S. J. Quinney College of Law's Kids' Court program see law.utah.edu/news/college-of-laws-kids-court-program-honored-with-pete-suazo-award-by-minority-bar-association/.

8. Over the years, it has been a challenge to obtain the achievement data that we need in order to compare academic outcomes. Among several reasons for this challenge is the fact that Utah is one of the states that has been very resistant to No Child Left Behind legislation and filed for waivers to not be included in the accountability measures.

Chapter 4

1. We modeled the Community Advocate Program after workshops that UNP (University Neighborhood Partners), the University of Utah's unit responsible for promoting and facilitating community-engaged research, had developed and implemented in Westside communities.

2. Over the years, Judith Flores Carmona, Nereida Oliva, Judi Perez-Torres, and Cinthia Cervantes-Castañeda worked closely with parents to access resources and facilitate meetings with school administrators. These graduate students also developed significant relationships with the parents that went beyond just working with them in the school, as they were often invited to their homes, quinceñeras, and bautismos, or trusted with conversations about migration stories, family concerns, and parenting wisdom.

3. Twelve of the 25 classroom teachers agreed to be interviewed about their perceptions and goals of the Adelante partnership, as well as their hopes for their students. Six of the teachers were from the dual-language immersion program and six were from the regular education program. Enrique's graduate students in a qualitative methods seminar interviewed the teachers. The graduate students were predominantly White female educators who were not associated with the Adelante partnership.

4. We previously implemented professional development focused on social justice and culturally relevant teaching. However, this work was minimal in the early years and had occurred only when an acting principal had prioritized it. Prior professional developments included facilitated workshops from individuals such as Norma Gonzalez, a curriculum specialist from Tucson Unified's former Mexican American Studies program, presenting "Towards a Pedagogy of Love and Humanization"; Dr. Audrey Thompson, presenting "Whiteness in the Classroom"; Mary Burbank, presenting "Understanding Our Roles as Activist-Minded Educators"; and Dr. Veronica Valdez and Dr. Juan Freire, presenting "Spanish Oral Language Development." In addition, Dr. Juan Freire collaborated with the

dual-immersion teachers to support culturally relevant pedagogy during the entire 2012–2013 academic year.

Chapter 5

1. The Center for Ethnic Student Affairs (CESA), originally created as the "Minority Center" in 1970, is currently a multifunctional student support program under the Office for Equity and Diversity. CESA plays a significant role on campus in the retention and graduation of students of color by providing student orientations, academic and personal counseling, tutoring, and academic programming.

2. Sponsored students were admitted under the university's Five Percent Policy, which allowed for 5% of any incoming class to be comprised of students who do not meet the admission index (a formula that includes high school GPA and ACT/SAT scores) or other admissions requirements.

3. Dr. Sonya Alemán was the faculty director of the program from 2012 to 2015, strengthening multiple aspects and developing the relationship with ethnic studies faculty.

4. Since the establishment of an ethnic studies major in 2011, 42% of the majors are former Diversity Scholars. And since the establishment of the Diversity Scholars Program in 2007, each year between 7% and 32% of the Diversity Scholars take one or more ethnic studies courses after completing the program (Alemán & Gaytán, 2016; Valles, 2016).

5. As we write this chapter, the university is conducting a formal review of the Diversity Scholars Program with the stated purpose of ensuring that no matter what leadership changes and program or funding shifts occur in the future, the Diversity Scholars program is protected and institutionalized via the Office of Equity and Diversity.

6. Over the years, the faculty members who have co-taught the courses have brought their disciplinary expertise to continuously renew, reshape, and improve the curriculum, yet the core of the course remains focused on the educational experiences of students of color.

7. Though the majority of the students completed their service learning with Adelante, 30%–40% of the remaining students mentored students at other sites. With varying levels of success and sustainability, these sites have included Black Butterflies, the American Indian Walk-In Center, Center for Ethnic Student Affairs, Calvary Baptist Academy of Excellence, Bryant Middle School, Mestizo Arts & Activism, Glendale Middle School Dreamkeepers, and Mana Academy Charter School.

8. Half of the Diversity Scholars have self-identified as Latin@, with Asian American students comprising the next largest proportion at 18%, followed by Pacific Islander and African American students both at approximately 8% (Valles, 2016). Bilingual or multilingual students have made up 60% of the total, with at least 80% of them being first-generation college students. Records approximate about 6–10% of Diversity Scholars have been undocumented (Alemán & Gaytán, 2016).

9. Our qualitative data collection strategies for this chapter included in-depth, one-on-one interviews, focus group interviews, and in-class and out-of-class discus-

sions and observations with faculty and mentors in the Diversity Scholars Program between 2007 and 2015. In addition, we draw from students' written and digital reflections that were built into the course syllabus.

10. The analysis that follows draws heavily from our 2009 *Harvard Educational Review* article in which we focus on the Latin@ student mentors. We have extended our analysis here to include the ethnic/racial diversity included among the mentors.

Chapter 6

1. Over the years we partnered with the Office of the President, Office of the Provost, University Neighborhood Partners (UNP), Office of Community Engagement, Office of Undergraduate Studies, the Bennion Center for Service Learning, Ethnic Studies Program, Gender Studies Program, Center for Ethnic Student Affairs, American Indian Resource Center, Office of the Assistant Vice President for Community Outreach, Youth Education, and a number of other academic units that provided time and support to our field trip, science camp, community garden, ballet folklórico, and mentoring programs.

2. Initially, graduate students wrote and translated most of the stories and took the photos. Later, teachers and students collaborated in contributing to the newsletter. As a parent, former journalist, and communications professor, Dr. Sonya Alemán volunteered to edit and do the layout for the monthly newsletters from 2008 to 2015.

Epilogue

1. To learn more about high school graduating seniors participating in a graduation walk through the halls of Jackson Elementary and local middle schools, see www. ksl.com/?sid=40051296&nid=148&title=what-we-became-west-high-grads-visit-former-schools-to-celebrate-and-inspiree.

REFERENCES

Acuña, R. (1988). *Occupied America: A history of Chicanos* (3rd ed.). New York, NY: Harper Collins.

Alemán, E., Jr. (2006). Is Robin Hood the "Prince of Thieves" or a pathway to equity? Applying Critical Race Theory to school finance political discourse. *Educational Policy, 20*(1), 113–142.

Alemán, E., Jr. (2007). Situating Texas school finance policy in a CRT framework: How "substantially equal" yields racial inequity. *Educational Administration Quarterly, 43*(5), 525–558.

Alemán, E., Jr. (2009a). LatCrit educational leadership and advocacy: Struggling over whiteness as property in Texas school finance. *Equity & Excellence in Education, 42*(2), 183–201.

Alemán, E., Jr. (2009b). Through the prism of critical race theory: Niceness and Latina/o leadership in the politics of education. *Journal of Latinos and Education, 8*(4), 290–311.

Alemán, E., Jr., & Alemán, S. M. (2010). Do Latin@ interests always have to "converge" with White interests? (Re)claiming racial realism and interest-convergence in critical race theory praxis. *Race Ethnicity and Education, 13*(1), 1–21.

Alemán, E., Jr., Delgado Bernal, D., & Mendoza, S. (2013). Critical race methodological tensions: Nepantla in our community-based praxis. In M. Lynn & A. Dixson (Eds.), *Handbook of Critical Race Theory in education* (pp. 325–338). New York, NY: Routledge.

Alemán, E., Jr., Pérez-Torres, J., & Oliva, N. (2013). *Adelante en Utah*: Dilemmas of leadership and college access in a university–school–community p artnership. *Journal of Cases in Educational Leadership, 16*(3), 7–30.

Alemán, E., Jr., & Rorrer, A. K. (2006). *Closing educational achievement gaps for Latino students in Utah: Initiating a policy discourse and framework*. Salt Lake City, UT: Utah Education Policy Center. Retrieved from uepc.utah.edu/_documents/UEPC-centro-achievement-gap.pdf

Alemán, S. M., & Gaytán, M. S. (2016). "It doesn't speak to me": Understanding student of color resistance to critical race pedagogy. *International Journal of Qualitative Studies in Education*. DOI: 10.1080/09518398.2016.1242801

Anzaldúa, G. (1987). *Borderlands/La Frontera: The new mestiza*. San Francisco, CA: Aunt Lute Books.

Anzaldúa, G. (2000). Toward a mestiza rhetoric. In A. L. Keating (Ed.), *Gloria Anzaldúa: Interviews/entrevistas* (pp. 251–280). New York, NY: Routledge.

Anzaldúa, G. (2002). Now let us shift . . . the path of conocimiento . . . inner works, public acts. In G. Anzaldúa & A. L. Keating (Eds.), *This bridge we call home: Radical visions for transformation* (pp. 540–578). New York, NY: Routledge.

Anzaldúa, G. (2005). Let us be the healing of the wound: The Coyolxauhqui imperative–La sombra y el sueno. In C. Joysmith & C. Lomas (Eds.), *One wound for another/Una herida por otra: Testimonios de Latin@s in the US through cyberspace* (pp. 92–103). Mexico City, Mexico: Universidad Nacional Autonoma de Mexico.

Auerbach, S. (2002). "Why do they give the good classes to some and not to others?": Latino parent narratives of struggle in a college access program. *Teachers College Record, 104*(7), 1369–1392.

Ayala, J. (2008). What is our work in the academy? In K. P. González & R. V. Padilla (Eds.), *Doing the public good: Latina/o scholars engage civic participation* (pp. 25–37). Sterling, VA: Stylus.

Ayala, J., Herrera, P., Jiménez, L., & Lara, I. (2006). Fiera, guambra, y karichina! Transgressing the borders of community and academy. In D. D. Bernal, C. A. Elenes, F. E. Godinez, & S. Villenas (Eds.), *Chicana/Latina education in everyday life: Feminista perspectives on pedagogy and epistemology* (pp. 261–280). Albany, NY: State University of New York Press.

Bell, D. A. (1992). Racial realism. *Connecticut Law Review, 24*(2), 363–379.

Bell, D. A. (1995). Racial realism. In K. Crenshaw, N. Gotanda, G. Peller, & K. Thomas (Eds.), *Critical race theory: The key writings that formed the movement* (pp. 302–312). New York, NY: The New Press.

Bell, D. A. (2004). *Silent covenants: Brown v. Board of Education and the unfulfilled hopes for racial reform*. Oxford, England: Oxford University Press.

Benson, L., & Harkavy, I. (2001). Leading the way to meaningful partnerships. *Principal Leadership, 2*(1), 54–58.

Benson, L., Harkavy, I., & Puckett, J. (2007). *Dewey's dream: Universities and democracies in an age of education reform*. Philadelphia, PA: Temple University Press.

Betsinger, A., García, S. B., & Guerra, P. (2001). Addressing teachers' beliefs about diverse students through staff development. *Journal of Staff Development, 22*(2), 24–27.

Biddle, B. J., & Berliner, D. C. (2002). *What the research says for unequal funding in America's schools*. Tempe, AZ: Arizona State University Education Policy Studies Laboratory. Retrieved from files.eric.ed.gov/fulltext/ED473409.pdf

Boncana, M. (2010). *Partnership, student achievement, and parental involvement in a Utah elementary: Multilevel growth curve and critical interpretive analyses* (Doctoral dissertation). The University of Utah.

Brady, K., Eatman, T., & Parker, L. (2000). To have or not to have? A preliminary analysis of higher education funding disparities in the post–*Ayers* v. *Fordice* era: Evidence from critical race theory. *Journal of Education Finance, 25*(3), 297–322.

Bulkeley, D. (2005, May 15). Minutemen focus on Utah: Group works at state level to halt illegal immigration. *Deseret Morning News*. Retrieved from www.deseretnews.com

Bulkeley, D. (2008, June 26). Poll: Most Utahns back tough immigration bill. *Deseret News*. Retrieved from www.deseretnews.com

Burciaga, R., & Tavares, A. (2006). Our pedagogy of sisterhood: A testimonio. In D. Delgado Bernal, C. A. Elenes, F. E. Godinez, & S. Villenas (Eds.), *Chicana/Latina education in everyday life: Feminista perspectives on pedagogy and epistemology* (pp. 133–142). Albany, NY: State University of New York.

Calderón, D. (2014). Anticolonial methodologies in education: Embodying land and indigeneity in Chicana feminisms. *Journal of Latino/Latin American Studies, 6*(2), 81–96.

Calderón, D., Delgado Bernal, D., Velez, V. N., Pérez Huber, L., & Malagon, M. C. (2012). A Chicana feminist epistemology revisited: Cultivating ideas a generation later. *Harvard Educational Review, 82*(4), 513–539.

Cammarota, J., & Romero, A. (2011). Participatory action research for high school students: Transforming policy, practice, and the personal with social justice education. *Education Policy, 25*(3), 488–506.

Cammarota, J., & Romero, A. (2014). *Raza studies: The public option for educational revolution*. Tucson, AZ: University of Arizona Press.

Carey, K. (2004). *The funding gap 2004: Many states still shortchange low-income and minority students*. Washington, DC: The Education Trust.

Cochran-Smith, M. (1991). Learning to teach against the grain. *Harvard Educational Review, 51*(3), 279–310.

Cochran-Smith, M. (2004). *Walking the road: Race, diversity, and social justice in teacher education*. New York, NY: Teachers College Press.

Collier, V. P., & Thomas, W. P. (2004). The astounding effectiveness of dual language education for all. *NABE Journal for Research and Practice, 2*(1), 1–20.

Crenshaw, K. W., Gotanda, N., Peller, G., & Thomas, K. (Eds.). (1995). *Critical race theory: The key writings that formed the movement*. New York, NY: The New Press.

Cruz, C. (2006). Toward an epistemology of a brown body. In D. Delgado Bernal, C. A. Elenes, F. E. Godínez, & S. Villenas (Eds.), *Chicana/Latina education in everyday life: Feminista perspectives on pedagogy and epistemology* (pp. 59–75). Albany, NY: State University of New York Press.

Cruz, C. (2013). LGBTQ youth of color video making as radical curriculum: A brother mourning his brother and a theory in the flesh. *Curriculum Inquiry, 43*(4), 441–460.

Darling-Hammond, L. (2007). The flat earth and education: How America's commitment to equity will determine our future. *Educational Researcher, 36*(6), 318–334.

Davis, M. R., & Archer, J. (2005, May 11). Complaint targets Utah NCLB law. *Education Week, 24*, 22.

Delgado, R., & Stefancic, J. (Eds.). (1998). *The Latino condition: A critical reader*. New York, NY: New York University Press.

Delgado, R., & Stefancic, J. (2001). *Critical Race Theory: An introduction.* New York, NY: New York University Press.

Delgado Bernal, D. (1998). Grassroots leadership reconceptualized: Chicana oral histories and the 1968 East Los Angeles school blowouts. *Frontiers, 19*(2), 113–142.

Delgado Bernal, D. (1999). Chicana/o education from the civil rights era to the present. In J. F. Moreno (Ed.), *The elusive quest for equality* (pp. 77–108). Cambridge, MA: Harvard Educational Review.

Delgado Bernal, D. (2001). Learning and living pedagogies of the home: The mestiza conciousness of Chicana students. *International Journal of Qualitative Studies in Education, 14*(5), 623–639.

Delgado Bernal, D. (2002). Critical race theory, Latino critical theory, and critical raced-gendered epistemologies: Recognizing students of color as holders and creators of knowledge. *Qualitative Inquiry, 8*(1), 105–126.

Delgado Bernal, D. (2008). La trenza de las identidades: Weaving together our personal, professional, and communal identities. In K. Gonzalez & R. Padilla (Eds.), *Doing the public good: Latina/o scholars engage civic participation* (pp. 135–148). Sterling, VA: Stylus.

Delgado Bernal, D., Alemán, E., Jr., & Flores Carmona, J. (2008). Negotiating and contesting transnational and transgenerational Latina/o cultural citizenship: Kindergarteners, their parents, and university students in Utah. *Social Justice, 35*(1), 28–49.

Delgado Bernal, D., Alemán, E., Jr., & Garavito, A. (2009). Latina/o undergraduate students mentoring Latina/o elementary students: A borderlands analysis of shifting identities and college persistence. *Harvard Educational Review, 79*(4), 560–585.

Delgado Bernal, D., & Villalpando, O. (2002). An apartheid of knowledge in academia: The struggle over the "legitimate" knowledge of faculty of color. *Equity & Excellence in Education, 35*(2), 169–180.

Delpit, L. (1995). *Other people's children: Cultural conflict in the classroom.* New York, NY: The New Press.

Denzin, N. K., & Lincoln, Y. S. (Eds.). (2003). *The landscape of qualitative research: Theories and issues* (2nd ed.). Thousand Oaks, CA: Sage Publications.

Denzin, N. K., & Lincoln, Y. S. (Eds.). (2005). *Sage handbook of qualitative research* (3rd ed.). Thousand Oaks, CA: Sage Publications.

Donato, R. (1997). *The other struggle for equal schools: Mexican Americans during the civil rights era.* Albany, NY: SUNY Press.

Duncan, G. A. (2002). Critical race theory and method: Rendering race in urban ethnographic research. *Qualitative Inquiry, 8*(1), 85–104.

Duncan-Andrade, J. (2009). Note to educators: Hope required when growing roses in concrete. *Harvard Educational Review, 79*(2), 181–194.

Duncan-Andrade, J., & Morrell, E. (2008). *The art of critical pedagogy: Possibilities for moving from theory to practice in urban schools.* New York, NY: Peter Lang.

Dyrness, A. (2008). Research for change versus research as change: Lessons from a Mujerista participatory research team. *Anthropology & Education Quarterly, 39*(1), 23–44.

Elenes, C. A. (2011). *Transforming borders: Chicana/o popular culture and pedagogy.* Lanham, MD: Lexington Books.

Espinoza, L., & Harris, A. P. (1998). Embracing the tar-baby: LatCrit theory and the sticky mess of race. *La Raza Law Journal, 10*(Spring), 1585–1644.

Facio, E., & Lara, I. (Eds.). (2014). *Fleshing the spirit: Spirituality and activism in Chicana, Latina, and Indigenous women's lives.* Tucson, AZ: University of Arizona Press.

Fierros, C., & Delgado Bernal, D. (2016). Vamos a platicar: The contours of platicas as methodology. *Chicana/Latina Studies, 15*(2), 98–121.

Flores Carmona, J. (2010). *Transgenerational educacion: Latina mothers' everyday pedagogies of cultural citizenship in Salt Lake City, Utah* (Doctoral dissertation). University of Utah.

Flores Carmona, J., & Delgado Bernal, D. (2012). Oral histories in the classroom: The Latina/o home as a pedagogical site. In C. E. Sleeter & E. Soriano Ayala (Eds.), *Building solidarity between schools and marginalized communities: International perspectives* (pp. 114–130). New York, NY: Teachers College Press.

Foley, D., & Valenzuela, A. (2008). Critical ethnography: The politics of collaboration. In N. K. Denzin & Y. S. Lincoln (Eds.), *The landscape of qualitative research* (pp. 287–310). Thousand Oaks, CA: Sage Publications.

Fránquiz, M. E., Avila, A., & Lewis, B. A. (2013). Engaging bilingual students in sustained literature study in central Texas. *Journal of Latino-Latin American Studies (JOLLAS), 5*(3), 142–155.

Freire, J. A. (2014). *Spanish-English dual language teacher beliefs and practices on culturally relevant pedagogy in a collaborative action research process* (Doctoral dissertation). University of Utah.

Freire, J. A. (2016). Nepantleras/os and their teachers in dual language education: Developing sociopolitical consciousness to contest language education policies. *Association of Mexican American Educators Journal, 10*(1), 36–52.

Gándara, P., & Contreras, F. (2009). *The Latino crisis: The consequences of failed social policies.* Cambridge, MA: Harvard University Press.

García, S., & Guerra, P. (2004). Deconstructing deficit thinking: Working with educators to create more equitable learning environments. *Education and Urban Society, 36*(2), 150–168.

Godinez, F. E. (2006). Haciendo que hacer: Braiding cultural knowledge into educational practices and policies. In D. D. Bernal, C. A. Elenes, F. E. Godinez, & S. Villenas (Eds.), *Chicana/Latina education in everyday life: Feminista perspectives on pedagogy and epistemology* (pp. 25–38). Albany, NY: State University of New York Press.

González, F. E. (1998). Formations of Mexicana ness: Trenzas de identidades multiples Growing up Mexicana : Braids of multiple identities. *International Journal of Qualitative Studies in Education, 11*(1), 81–102.

González, N., Moll, L. C., Tenery, M. F., Rivera, A., Rendon, P., Gonzales, R., & Amanti, C. (1995). Funds of knowledge for teaching in Latino households. *Urban Education, 29*(4), 443–470.

Guajardo, M. A., & Guajardo, F. J. (2004). The impact of *Brown* on the brown of South Texas: A micropolitical perspective on the education of Mexican Americans in a South Texas community. *American Educational Research Journal, 41*(3), 501–526.

Guajardo, M. A., Guajardo, F. J., & Del Carmen Casaperalta, E. (2008). Transformative education: Chronicling a pedagogy for social change. *Anthropology and Education Quarterly, 39*(1), 3–22.

Haney-López, I. F. (1998). Race, ethnicity, nationhood: Race, ethnicity, erasure: The salience of race to LatCrit Theory. *La Raza Law Journal, 10*, 1143–1211.

Harkavy, I. (1998, January). *School-community-university partnerships: Effectively integrating community building and education reform*. Paper presented at Connecting Community Building and Education Reform: Effective School, Community, University Partnerships, Washington, DC. Retrieved from www.community-wealth. org/_pdfs/articles-publications/universities/paper-harkavy.pdf

Hernández-Truyol, B. E. (1998). Building bridges: Latinas and Latinos at the crossroads. In R. Delgado & J. Stefancic (Eds.), *The Latino condition: A critical reader* (pp. 24–31). New York, NY: New York University Press.

hooks, b. (1989). *Talking back: Thinking feminist, thinking black*. Cambridge, MA: South End Press.

Jacobi, M. (1991). Mentoring and undergraduate academic success: A literature review. *Review of Educational Research, 61*(4), 505–532.

Jarsky, K. M., McDonough, P. M., & Núñez, A. M. (2009). Establishing a college culture in secondary schools through P–20 collaboration: A case study. *Journal of Hispanic Higher Education, 8*(4), 357–373.

Jiménez, K. P. (2014). The making of a queer Latina cartoon: Pedagogies of border, body, and home. *Journal of Latino-Latin American Studies (JOLLAS), 6*(2), 125–134.

Keating, A. L. (2006). From borderlands and new mestizas to nepantlas and nepantleras: Anzaldúan theories for social change. *Human Architecture: Journal of the Sociology of Self Knowledge, 4*(3, 5–16).

Kohli, R., & Pizarro, M. (2016). Fighting to educate our own: Teachers of color, relational accountability and the struggle for racial justice. *Equity and Excellence in Education, 49*(1), 72–84.

Kohli, R., & Solórzano, D. G. (2012). Teachers, please learn our names!: Racial microaggressions and the K–12 classroom. *Race Ethnicity and Education, 15*(4), 441–462.

Kozol, J. (1991). *Savage inequalities*. New York, NY: Harper Perrenial.

Kozol, J. (2012). *Fire in the ashes: Twenty-five years among the poorest children in America*. New York, NY: Broadway Books.

Ladson-Billings, G. (1998). Just what is critical race theory and what's it doing in a *nice* field like education. *Qualitative Studies in Education, 11*(1), 7–24.

Ladson-Billings, G. (2001). *Crossing over to Canaan: The journey of new teachers in diverse classrooms*. San Francisco, CA: Jossey-Bass, Inc.

Ladson-Billings, G. (2006). From the achievement gap to the educational debt: Understanding achievement in the U.S. schools. *Educational Researcher, 35*(7), 3–12.

Ladson-Billings, G. (2009). *The dreamkeepers: Successful teachers of African American children* (2nd ed.). San Francisco, CA: John Wiley & Sons.

Ladson-Billings, G., & Donner, J. (2005). The moral activist role of critical race theory scholarship. In N. K. Denzin & Y. S. Lincoln (Eds.), *Sage handbook on qualitative research* (3rd ed., pp. 279–301). Thousand Oaks, CA: Sage Publications.

Ladson-Billings, G., & Tate, W. (1997). Toward a critical race theory in education. *Teachers College Record, 97*(1), 47.

Lara, I. (2002). Healing sueños for academia. In G. E. Anzaldúa & A. L. Keating (Eds.), *This bridge we call home* (pp. 433–438). New York, NY: Routledge.

Lynn, M., & Dixson, A. D. (Eds.). (2013). *Handbook of critical race theory in education*. New York, NY: Routledge.

Lynn, R. (2005, April 20). Utah bucks feds on schools. *Salt Lake Tribune*. Retrieved from archive.sltrib.com/story.php?ref=/ci_2669791

Mendoza, S. (2014). The Adelante oral history project as a site of decolonial potential in transforming school curriculums. *Regeneración Tlacuilolli: UCLA Raza Studies Journal, 1*(1).

Mendoza, S. (2015). *Reimagining education with nepantlera/o elementary-aged youth through Anzaldua and critical youth studies* (Doctoral dissertation). University of Utah.

Montejano, D. (1987). *Anglos and Mexicans in the making of Texas, 1836–1986*. Austin, TX: University of Texas Press.

Montoya, M. E. (1994). Mascaras, trenzas, y grenas: Un/masking the self while un/braiding Latina stories and legal discourse. *Chicano-Latino Law Review, 15*(1), 1–37.

Moraga, C. (2000). *Loving in the war years: Lo que nunca pasó por sus labios* (2nd ed.). Boston, MA: South End Press.

Morales, S. (2016). *Fostering critical counterspaces in the borderlands: Engaging Latin@ youth in Chican@ studies* (Doctoral dissertation). University of Utah.

Morales, S., Mendoza, S., & Delgado Bernal, D. (2016). Education in nepantla: A Chicana feminist approach to engaging Latina/o elementary youth in ethnic studies. In D. M. Sandoval, A. J. Ratcliff, T. L. Buenavista, & J. R. Marín (Eds.), *"White" washing American education: The new culture wars in ethnic studies* (pp. 67–93). Santa Barbara, CA: Praeger.

Oakes, J. (1985). *Keeping track: How schools structure inequality*. New Haven, CT: Yale University Press.

Oliva, N., Pérez, J. C., & Parker, L. (2013). Educational policy contradictions: A LatCrit perspective on undocumented Latino students. In M. Lynn & A. D. Dixson (Eds.), *Handbook of Critical Race Theory in Education* (pp. 140–152). New York, NY: Routledge.

Olivos, E. M. (2007). *The power of parents: A critical perspective of bicultural parent involvement in public schools*. New York, NY: Peter Lang.

Orfield, G., Kucsera, J., & Siegel-Hawley, G. (2012). *E pluribus . . . separation: Deepening double segregation for more students.* Los Angeles, CA: Civil Rights Project. Retrieved from civilrightsproject.ucla.edu/research/k-12-education/integration-and-diversity/mlk-national/e-pluribus...separation-deepening-double-segregation-for-more-students/orfield_epluribus_revised_omplete_2012.pdf

Pérez Huber, L. (2009). Challenging racist nativist framing: Acknowledging the community cultural wealth of undocumented Chicana college students to reframe the immigration debate. *Harvard Educational Review, 79*(4), 704–729.

Pérez Huber, L. (2015). "Como una jaula de oro" (It's like a golden cage): The impact of DACA and the California DREAM Act on undocumented Chicanas/Latinas. *Chicana/oLatina/o Law Review, 33*(1), 91–128.

Pérez Huber, L., Benavides Lopez, C., Malagon, M. C., Velez, V., & Solórzano, D. G. (2008). Getting beyond the "symptom," acknowledging the "disease": Theorizing racist nativism. *Contemporary Justice Review, 11*(1), 39–51.

Perlich, P. S. (2002). *Utah minorities: The story told by 150 years of census data.* Salt Lake City: University of Utah. Retrieved from www.bebr.utah.edu/Documents/studies/Utah_Minorities.pdf

Perlich, P. S. (2004). Immigrants transform Utah: Entering a new era of diversity. *Utah Economic and Business Review, 64*(5 & 6), 1–16.

Perlich, P. S. (2008). Utah's demographic transformation: A view into the future. *Utah Economic and Business Review, 68*(3), 1–11.

Pizarro, M. (2005). *Chicanas and Chicanos in school: Racial profiling, identity battles and empowerment.* Austin, TX: University of Texas Press.

Prieto, L., & Villenas, S. (2012). Toward pedagogies from nepantla: Testimonio, Chicana/Latina feminisms, and teacher education classrooms. *Equity and Excellence in Education, 45*(3), 411–429.

Russel y Rodríguez, M. (1998). Confronting anthropology's silencing praxis: Speaking of/from a Chicana consciousness. *Qualitative Inquiry, 4*(1), 15–40.

San Miguel, G., & Valencia, R. R. (1998). From the Treaty of Guadalupe Hidalgo to *Hopwood*: The educational plight and struggle of Mexican Americans in the Southwest. *Harvard Educational Review, 68*(3), 353–412.

Sanchez, J. W. (2007, February 13). Utah House passes immigration enforcement bill. *Salt Lake Tribune.* Retrieved from www.sltrib.com

Sanchez, J. W. (2008, February 12). House votes to abolish driver cards for undocumented immigrants; Senate test next. *Salt Lake Tribune.* Retrieved from www.sltrib.com

Sanchez, J. W., & Lyon, J. (2006, April 10). Latinos march en masse to urge fairness, respect. *Salt Lake Tribune.* Retrieved from www.sltrib.com

Sanderson, H. L. (2005). *Trends and patterns of Utah's white and Hispanic 4th grade students compared to the nation: An NAEP achievement gap analysis.* Salt Lake City: Utah State Office of Education.

Shakur, T. (1999). *The rose that grew from concrete.* New York, NY: Pocket Books.

Sleeter, C. E. (2001). Preparing teachers for culturally diverse schools research and the overwhelming presence of whiteness. *Journal of Teacher Education, 52*(2), 94–106.

Smith, L. T. (1999). *Decolonizing methodologies: Research and indigenous peoples.* New York, NY: Zed Books.

Solórzano, A. (1998). Struggle over memory: The roots of the Mexican Americans in Utah, 1776 through the 1850s. *Aztlán, 23*(2), 81–118.

Solórzano, A. (2005). At the gates of the kingdom: Latino immigrants in Utah, 1900 to 2003. In E. M. Gozdziak & S. F. Martin (Eds.), *Beyond the gateway: Immigrants in a changing America* (pp. 177–212). Lanham, MD: Lexington Books.

Solórzano, A. (2006). Latinos' education in Mormon Utah, 1910–1960. *Latino Studies, 4,* 282–301.

Solórzano, D. G. (1998). Critical race theory, racial and gender microaggressions, and the experiences of Chicana and Chicano scholars. *International Journal of Qualitative Studies in Education, 11,* 121–136.

Solórzano, D. G., & Delgado Bernal, D. (2001). Examining transformational resistance through a critical race and LatCrit theory framework: Chicana and Chicano students in an urban context. *Urban Education, 36*(3), 308–342.

Solórzano, D. G., & Yosso, T. J. (2001a). Critical race and LatCrit theory and method: Counter-storytelling. *Qualitative Studies in Education, 14*(4), 471–495.

Solórzano, D. G., & Yosso, T. J. (2001b). From racial stereotyping and deficit discourse: Toward a critical race theory in teacher education. *Multicultural Education, 9*(1), 2–8.

Stovall, D. O. (2005). A challenge to traditional theory: Critical race theory, African-American community organizers, and education. *Discourse: Studies in the Cultural Politics of Education, 26*(1), 95–108.

Stovall, D. O. (2016). *Born out of struggle: Critical race theory, school creation, and the politics of interruption.* Albany, NY: SUNY Press.

Stovall, D. O., Lynn, M., Danley, L., & Martin, D. (2009). Critical race praxis in education. *Race Ethnicity and Education, 12*(2), 131–132.

Tatum, B. D. (1999). *Assimilation blues: Black families in a White community.* New York, NY: Basic Books.

Téllez, M. (2005). Doing research at the borderlands: Notes from a Chicana feminist ethnographer. *Chicana/Latina Studies, 4*(2), 46–70.

Teranishi, R. T., & Pazich, L. B. (2013). The inclusion and representation of Asian Americans and Pacific Islanders in America's equity agenda in higher education. In M. Lynn & A. D. Dixson (Eds.), *Handbook of Critical Race Theory in education* (pp. 204–215). New York, NY: Routledge.

Tijerina Revilla, A. (2004). Muxerista pedagogy: Raza womyn teaching social justice through student activism. *The High School Journal, 87*(4), 80–94.

Tintiangco-Cubales, A., Daus-Magbual, R., & Daus-Magbual, R. (2010). Pin@y educational partnerships: A counter-pipeline to create critical educators. *AAPI Nexus: Policy, Practice and Community, 8*(1), 75–102.

Tuck, E., & Yang, K. W. (2012). Decolonization is not a metaphor. *Decolonization: Indigeneity, Education & Society, 1*(1), 1–40.

Urrieta, L., Jr. (2009). *Working from within: Chicana and Chicano activist educators in white-stream schools.* Tucson, AZ: University of Arizona Press.

U.S. Census Bureau. (2015). *Public education finances: 2013* (G13-ASPEF). Washington, DC: U.S. Government Printing Office.

U.S. Census Bureau. (2016). *Public education finances: 2014*(G14-ASPEF). Washington, DC: U.S. Government Printing Office.

Utah State Office of Education. (2012). *Fall enrollment by grade, gender, and race* [Data file]. Retrieved from www.schools.utah.gov/data/Reports/Enrollment-Demographics.aspx

Valdés, F. (1997). Under construction—LatCrit consciousness, community, and theory. *California Law Review, 85,* 1087–1142.

Valencia, R. R. (2008). *Chicano students and the courts: The Mexican American legal struggle for educational equity.* New York, NY: New York University Press.

Valencia, R. R., & Black, M. S. (2002). "Mexican Americans don't value education!"—On the basis of the myth, mythmaking, and debunking. *Journal of Latinos and Education, 1*(2), 81–102.

Valencia, R. R., & Solórzano, D. G. (1997). Contemporary deficit thinking. In R. R. Valencia (Ed.), *The evolution of deficit thinking: Educational thought and practice* (pp. 72–95). London, England: The Falmer Press.

Valenzuela, A. (1999). *Subtractive schooling: U.S.-Mexican youth and the politics of caring.* Albany, NY: State University of New York Press.

Valenzuela, A. (Ed.). (2004). *Leaving children behind: How Texas-style accountability fails Latino youth.* Albany, NY: State University of New York Press.

Valenzuela, A. (Ed.). (2016). *Growing critically conscious teachers: A social justice curriculum for educators of Latino/a youth.* New York, NY: Teachers College Press.

Valles, B. (2016). *Diversity Scholar retention and graduation* [Data file], concatenated, 2007–2016. Salt Lake City, UT: University of Utah Office for Equity & Diversity, Office for Research & Assessment.

Valles, B., & Villalpando, O. (2013). A critical race policy analysis of the school-to-prison pipeline for Chicano males. In M. Lynn & A. D. Dixson (Eds.), *Handbook of Critical Race Theory in education* (pp. 260–269). New York, NY: Routledge.

Villalpando, O. (2010). Latinos/as in higher education: Eligibility, enrollment, and educational attainment. In E. G. Murillo, S. Villenas, R. T. Galván, J. S. Muñoz, C. Martínez, & M. Machado-Casas (Eds.), *Handbook of Latinos and education: Theory, research and practice* (pp. 232–249). New York, NY: Routledge.

Villenas, S. (1996). The colonizer/colonized Chicana ethnographer: Identity, marginalization, and co-optation in the field. *Harvard Educational Review, 66*(4), 711–732.

Walker, S. C., & Taub, D. J. (2001). Variables correlated with satisfaction with a mentoring relationship in first-year college students and their mentors. *Journal of the First-Year Experience and Students in Transition, 13*(1), 47–67.

Yosso, T. J. (2006). *Critial race counterstories along the Chicana/Chicano educational pipeline.* New York, NY: Routledge.

INDEX

About the Authors

Enrique Alemán, Jr., is professor and chair in the Department of Educational Leadership & Policy Studies at the University of Texas at San Antonio. His research agenda includes studying the impact of educational policies on Latina/o and Chicana/o students and communities, the utilization of Critical Race Theory (CRT) and Latina/o Critical Theory (LatCrit) frameworks in educational research, and the application of community-based research methods as a way of informing the creation of pathways to higher education. Dr. Alemán has published articles in *Harvard Educational Review, Race Ethnicity and Education, Educational Administration Quarterly,* and *Equity, Excellence and Education,* as well as numerous chapters in edited books. As co-founder and former co-director of both the *Westside Pathways Project* and the *Adelante Partnership,* he led efforts to develop and implement college awareness and expectation programs for historically underrepresented students and communities in Salt Lake City, Utah.

Dolores Delgado Bernal is professor in the Department of Education, Culture, and Society and the Division of Ethnic Studies at the University of Utah. Her research encompasses two interrelated areas of study. Within the first, she explores critical raced-gendered epistemologies and pedagogies. In doing so, she looks to critical theoretical models to better understand and disrupt the sociopolitical, gendered, and racialized contexts that frame Chicanx educational experiences. Her second related area of interest is in methodology and its application in community-engaged and justice-based research. She is coeditor of *Chicana/Latina Education in Everyday Life: Feminista Perspectives on Pedagogy and Epistemology,* which received the American Educational Studies Association Critics Choice Award, and coeditor of *Chicana/Latina Testimonios: Methodologies, Pedagogies, and Political Urgency.* She has published in *Harvard Educational Review, Chicana/Latina Studies,* and the *International Journal of Qualitative Studies,* among other journals.

Ruby Chacón is a community artist/muralist from Salt Lake City, Utah. Her work is influenced by the values of her family and community members,

125

who have survived some of life's harshest realities with grace, courage, humor, and collaboration. The cover art is a reflection of these familial and communal strengths. Chacón currently resides in Sacramento, California, where she continues her work. www.rubychacon.com